RESURRECTION of a
NATION

RESURRECTION of a
NATION

Solving the Energy, Financial, &
Political Crisis in America

KRIS AXHOJ & JOHN P. WALKER

authorHOUSE®

AuthorHouse™
1663 Liberty Drive
Bloomington, IN 47403
www.authorhouse.com
Phone: 1-800-839-8640

First published by AuthorHouse 8/10/2010

ISBN: 978-1-4520-2354-0 (e)
ISBN: 978-1-4520-2353-3 (sc)
ISBN: 978-1-4520-2352-6 (hc)

Library of Congress Control Number: 2010906695

Printed in the United States of America
Bloomington, Indiana

This book is printed on acid-free paper.

Goal of this book

To educate the American public on the current energy, environmental, financial, and political situations and to identify logical solutions that can be implemented immediately. This book stands above political agendas and is written for the betterment of our Country no matter what political view you hold.

Dedication

To our families and Creator who has abundantly
blessed us and this beautiful Country.

Introduction

About three years ago, John had a dream - a common sense way to restore America to financial prosperity. At the time, he had no idea if the plan was viable or not. He began to research all the possible obstacles to see if his ideas were practical. He concluded that not only was the plan viable but necessary.

John pitched the concept to over five hundred business associates throughout the following two years and was met with resounding applause and urgency to create a vehicle to put the plan into action. He began to reach out to news agencies and talk shows, and after one interview, his phone and e-mail almost melted down from the responses of Americans who wanted to implement the plan sooner rather than later. John was not sure how to do this.

Like any other American, John began calling Senators and Congress members to help implement this plan of action. To his discouragement, these folks did not respond favorably, nor did they have any urgency. To make matters worse, many of the people responsible in the US Government were acting as the primary obstacle to the solution.

John and Kris met at their sons' soccer match. After discussing the plan and exchanging ideas on energy, sustainability and politics, they decided to put this down on paper and get it directly into the hands of the American people. What you are now reading is the result of many hours of collaborative research, analysis, and editing.

Proverbs 29:18 says, "Where there is no vision, the people perish." This book is designed to educate readers about America's crisis and present vision for a practical solution that can be implemented now. John and Kris are not politically oriented but results-oriented and are presenting a logical solution for America to implement. They are presenting facts that will cut through the veil of misinformation. The solutions are logical and can be easily accepted as a way of helping our great country regardless of political views.

John and Kris are not receiving funding from any special interest groups or companies with an agenda. It is very important you know this prior to reading this work because any attempt by them for financial gain while hurting the common good of the United States would make this research null and void.

The first two chapters of the book are intended to educate the reader on our nation's current energy scenario and alternatives recommended to remedy the energy crisis. Chapter three presents environmental issues and some of the forces behind the movements. The fourth and fifth chapters discuss our national debt and some thoughts on restructuring the government. The first five chapters will help you understand some of the major issues facing our country. Once America begins to prosper under the proposed solution, our country needs to take its excesses and satisfy its commitments. This book will present the arguments, define the crisis and propose a solution.

The authors' goal is to give you a vision that is factual, a compass with direction, and an urgency that if ignored will continue to lead our nation into financial ruin. America can no longer follow the course of least resistance.

Table of Contents

1. America's Current Energy Synopsis   1
    a. America's Energy Consumption   2
    b. Electric Power   3
    c. Fuel Energy Costs   4
    d. Where the Profits Are   5
    e. Who is Supplying America's Oil?   6

2. Cost of Renewable Energy   11
    a. Cost of Wind   13
    b. Cost for Solar   14
    c. Cost for Biomass   16
    d. Hydropower   17
    e. Cost for Nuclear   18
    f. National Smart Power Grid   20
    g. Conservation   21

3. Environmentalist or Imperialists?   25
    a. Global Warming History   26
    b. Scientific Letter of Skepticism   27
    c. Data and Analysis   31
    d. "Climate-Gate"   32
    e. The CO2 Issue   33
    f. Hidden Agendas   35

4. The US National Debt   39
    a. History   40
    b. The True Debt   43
    c. Who Owns the Debt   44
    d. Impact of Debt on Economy   46

5. Government Overhaul   49
    a. Purpose of Government   50
    b. Differing Government Views   51
    c. Term Limits   54

d.	Government Salaries	55
e.	Restructuring Ideas	58
f.	Representative Overhead	60
g.	Who Should Vote	61
6.	**The Crisis**	**65**
a.	Paths Of Discoveries	66
	i. Local Representation:	66
	ii. Senate Subcommittee on Energy:	67
	iii. Department of Energy (DOE):	67
b.	Climate Change	73
c.	Process of Status Quo:	73
7.	**The Solution**	**77**
a.	Where The Resources Are	78
b.	Jobs Impact	79
c.	Implementation	80
d.	Benefits from Solution	82
8.	**Where we go from here**	**85**

CHAPTER 1

America's Current Energy Synopsis

*It is evident that the fortunes of the world's human population,
for better or for worse, are inextricably interrelated
with the use that is made of energy resources.*

-M. King Hubbert, Resources and Man, 1969

The purpose of this chapter is to understand our country's energy consumption. We will explore the nation's current landscape of energy usage and then analyze the financials behind moving to clean energy in the next chapter. Let's see how dependent we are on fossil fuels and who is supplying our energy needs. We will briefly look at the Department of Energy and how it has helped us over the last thirty-three years of its existence. Finally, we will look at our imports and national security.

In bullet point format, we will explore:
- America's Energy Consumption
- What Powers Electricity
- Fuel Energy Costs
- Where are the Profits
- Who is Supplying America's Oil

America's Energy Consumption

There is no doubt America is currently based on a fossil fuel energy system. America's industry has its antennas up to move toward cleaner energy, but the conversion is expensive without government subsidies. The US Government is helping with tax incentives (lost revenue for the country) to help move this popular clean energy movement along. Even with all these intentions, it will take a long time to convert the country from fossil fuels. Take a look at the table below showing the current energy consumption breakdown by supply category:

US Current Energy Consumption Breakdown:

37.1% - Petroleum (ethanol fuel is included in "Renewable Energy.")
23.8% - Natural Gas
22.5% - Coal
8.5% - Nuclear Electric Power
7.3% - Renewable Energy Comprised of:
       1% - Solar PV
       5% - Geothermal
       6% - Waste
       7% - Wind
       19% - Biofuels
       28% - Wood (i.e. bamboo)
       34% - Hydroelectric Power

From the Department of Energy *Annual Energy Review 2008*

The dependence on fossil fuels in the US is - *Eighty Three Percent!* Logistically, that is a lot of energy to displace with "clean" energy. If we leave Natural Gas in the mix as an option for clean energy (accepted by some) but subtract out Petroleum and Coal, *Sixty Percent* of our energy will need to be replaced by renewable energy. This is not a stagnant number because the US Energy demand continues to increase. The energy consumption increased five percent in the last ten years. The strides to convert to clean "Renewable" energy equal only eight percent of the US total energy consumption after many years of technology advances. Like it or not, America has a long way to go to get rid of its fossil fuel dependency. So what are we going to do in the interim for our energy needs while we are waiting for renewable energy to become more affordable?

Electric Power

It is funny to hear people say we need to convert to electric energy so we will get rid of our fossil fuel dependency. Interestingly, most of the electricity generated in our country is not from renewable energy as the majority of people think. The great dams are not generating the majority of the electricity used for our consumption...coal is. The following table illustrates the fuels behind America's electrical power plants:

"Clean" Electricity is Powered by the following Fuels:

1% - Petroleum
23% - Natural Gas
45% - Coal
20% - Nuclear Electric Power
7% - Hydroelectric Power
4% - Other Renewable Energy

DOE (Electric Power Monthly with data for October 2009)

Electricity is not so clean considering sixty nine percent is fueled by fossil fuels. Coal has the environmentalists up in arms, but with newer "scrubbing" processes, staged combustion processes and now the processes of gasification, technologies exist that minimize pollutants before they can escape into the environment. All coal facilities built after 1978 had to have scrubbers installed to filter out sulfur pollutants.

Just a note on natural gas: It is the cleanest of all the fossil fuels and burns efficiently. Natural gas is composed primarily of methane. The byproducts of burning natural gas are carbon dioxide and water vapor - the same compounds we exhale when we breathe. Not too bad for the environment.

Believing our current electric grid will allow us to become energy independent and take the US off fossil fuels using "Renewable Energy" is not the total answer at this time. There are major benefits of using electric power. Almost all the fuel used to power electricity is harvested right here in the US, it is extremely inexpensive, and there is lots of it. We have plenty of domestic coal and gas to power electricity...essentially keeping dollars in America's economy.

Fuel Energy Costs

We have looked at the types and amount of energy the US is currently using. Let's look at the cost of generating energy from each fuel source to see which one is most efficient. Availability and costs of energy are extremely important to the American economy. As energy prices increase, the economy slows - elementary supply and demand.

The two main costs associated with energy, with traditional fuels or renewable sources, are infrastructure and harvesting/distribution. Infrastructure, which will be explored in the next chapter, can be extremely expensive depending on the technology and fuel type. After the infrastructure is built, the variable costs of harvesting the energy and its distribution are associated with every unit of energy produced.

The infrastructure, harvesting, and distribution systems for fossil fuels have been established and accepted for the longest period of time. The newer Renewable Energies (outside of wood and hydroelectric) are becoming more affordable as demand continues to grow, but are only practical when incentives, usually government incentives, make up the cost difference.

The latest published data by the Department of Energy show the costs per sector of energy:

Energy Costs
(Cost in 1970 Nominal Dollars per Million Btu by Energy Sector):
$17.89 - Petroleum
$9.62 - Natural Gas
$1.78 - Coal
$0.44 - Nuclear Electric Power
$3.18 – BioFuels

Energy Information Administration, "State Energy Data 2006: Prices and Expenditures"

Isn't it amazing! The most expensive cost is from the largest commodity used in America's energy consumption: petroleum. It just makes sense to target this commodity to relieve pressure on the US economy and national security. Why have we not worked on this issue before? The obvious answer is to increase America's *affordable* energy supply to eliminate the need to import oil.

Where the Profits Are

Most people have an opinion that the oil companies are raking in tremendous profits. We hear the total amount of money earned by these companies and the numbers sound staggering. Actually, the oil companies made only a modest 5.4% profit in 2009 when most manufacturing companies made around 8%. Understand most of these companies are publicly traded on the stock market, so investors (international and domestic) are also participating in earned profits. Investors seeking short-term and long-term financial gains have made oil a driving force in America's society and financial strategy. The numbers speak for themselves as to who has the power in energy production:

Major US Companies' Profitability in Billion Nominal Dollars:

$62.7   - Petroleum
$8.8   - Natural Gas
$.8 - Coal, Renewable Energy, Nuclear Electric Power

DOE (Major U.S. Energy Companies' Net Income, 1974-2007)

Oil has been a major force in our society and, as you can see from the US' dependence, it is not going to stop overnight. The profitability of the oil companies seem huge, but the companies have to be very large in order to be competitive considering the infrastructure it takes to run that type of operation. Oil has capital to invest in new areas for drilling and resources to make their profits without government incentives. Businesses create profits and profits are needed for America to prosper. Profits are just a telling sign of who is giving the consumers what they want at a price they will pay.

Who is Supplying America's Oil?

America has one of the highest per capita usages of energy in the world. The productivity of America is staggering as we out-produce by 3.5 times the Gross Domestic Product (GDP) of second place Japan and a very close third place China (2008 numbers as represented by World Development Indicators database, World Bank, 7 October 2009). America has led the world's economy basically since the industrial revolution in the early 1900's. However, in the 1970's it was obvious that the United States was hamstrung by oil producing countries, and that our first "Energy Crisis" during the Carter administration was a wake-up call that America needed to protect its economy and security. In 1977, the Department of Energy was formed with the following mission (outside of their nuclear responsibilities):

"To advance the national, economic, and energy security of the United States; to promote scientific and technological innovation in support of that mission;"

From the Department of Energy (DOE) Web site

Let's see how America is doing with the help of the DOE.

Total Imports of Petroleum (Top 15 Countries)
(Thousand Barrels per Day)

COUNTRY	YTD 2009
CANADA	2,464
MEXICO	1,234
NIGERIA *	804
SAUDI ARABIA *	1,012
VENEZUELA *	1,078
ALGERIA *	488
RUSSIA	554
IRAQ *	450
VIRGIN ISLANDS	276
ANGOLA *	460
COLOMBIA	278
UNITED KINGDOM	245
BRAZIL	307
KUWAIT *	187
AZERBAIJAN	75

*OPEC Countries
The data in the tables above exclude oil imports into U.S. territories.

US Energy Information Administration December 2009 Import Highlights: February 25, 2010

As of October 2009, the United States produced only thirty-nine percent of its oil and imported *sixty-one percent*. Our economy is not safe when it is controlled by foreign oil.

Why would America pay for expensive fuels that are mostly imported? It is very clear America's economic machine was brought up on oil and is now very dependent on it. Unfortunately, this monster continues to feed on America's economy, creating the largest wealth drain of any country in history. Additionally, if OPEC wants to choke our economy again, all they have to do is hold back on exports to our country.

Just to make this perfectly clear, America imports to the tune of over *eight hundred million dollars per day*. That is over *three hundred Billion dollars per year* - money leaving America in the greatest transfer of wealth in history. To make matters worse, many of the countries from which we purchase oil are undermining the United States with the very money we are spending on their oil. How crazy is that?

More than *one hundred Billion dollars per year* is going to countries that do not like the United States and would support terrorist activities against America's citizens. This wealth transfer is boosting countries that would destroy the hand that feeds them. This is not too smart considering our country spends *billions* of dollars fighting terrorist groups around the world that are partially funded through oil profits. So, we fund the people who do not like our country, and then we fund our troops to protect us from the terrorists we just funded. There is a "fund-a-mental" problem with this. We are playing with our national security.

Our understanding is that there is around three to four days' worth of food stored at the grocery store. If a hostile force shuts down the Persian Gulf and our oil supply is shut off from that region, America could get very hungry within a week. If there is no fuel to transport food around the country and over the seas, it would cause havoc in our country just on the logistics level - not to mention fueling our military for national security.

Is the Department of Energy having any success making America stronger, or are their 16,000 employees and over 100,000 contractors just giving us pretty graphs and following the media trends on environmental issues? The government might have given a half-hearted plan for 2030 or 2050, but 33 years after the DOE was set up, we are no better off. There are no teeth behind their plans, just expensive planning and data collection that pacify people into believing the department is a benefit to our society. It is an unsuccessful government agency that is a tumor on the American taxpayer. We will be talking more about the Department of Energy later.

Summary

The US is very dependent on oil. It will take a long time to displace thirty eight percent of our energy consumption. The Department of Energy was established 33 years ago to help America become independent from foreign oil. In 2009, America was still importing sixty one percent of its oil. The facts suggest that our nation needs to act *now* in a responsible way to do what is financially plausible in our new economy. We need practical actions *now* to sustain America's economy and stop our dependencies on foreign oil. America must become energy independent.

CHAPTER 2

Cost of Renewable Energy

Beware of little expenses; a small leak will sink a great ship.

Benjamin Franklin

The government is pushing for renewable energy as basically the only solution to our energy independence. America is in a critical period in which our economy is suffering and the national debt is rising at an unprecedented rate. The government is spending enormous amounts of money on funding renewable research and development, but perhaps it should let free enterprise produce the best results? How many government efforts are productive, efficient and/or profitable?

There is a need for healthy renewable energy as the total world consumption of marketed energy is projected to increase by forty-four percent from 2006 to 2030 (**DOE (Report #:DOE/EIA-0484(2009))**. Why not let the free market, which has made America great, take its course. As the need grows, innovations and alternative supplies will increase to solve the problems of scarcity.

Environmentalists and the government are calling for renewable energy now. The cost to implement renewable energy infrastructure is tremendous. As we saw in the last chapter, renewable energies are currently only *eight percent* of the total picture of America's consumption. This energy sector would have to grow another *sixty percent* to eliminate petroleum and coal energy production. The amount of capital to convert sixty percent of our energy needs is way too staggering, so we are just going to analyze what it would take to remove our foreign oil dependency. To stop the transfer of wealth to foreign oil suppliers, America would have to replace *twenty-two percent* of its total energy consumption. Just for kicks, we will also do some number crunching to get rid of the *twelve percent* of imports to the United States being supplied by countries considered hostile toward us.

To understand the renewable energy options, we will look at the technology and costs for implementing "Clean" energies. In this chapter, we will look at:
+ Wind
+ Solar
+ Biomass
+ Hydroelectric
+ Nuclear
+ National Smart Power Grid
+ Conservation

This chapter will feel like a textbook because of the number crunching. It is designed for you to understand how expensive these renewable technologies are today. The numbers illustrate what it would take to replace imported petroleum with renewable energy. In each category we will talk about the infrastructure costs, variable costs, payback and barrier-to-entry into the market.

Cost of Wind

Wind Energy has become an important part of renewable energy. America now leads the world in wind generation and in 2008 experienced a fifty percent growth rate (World Wind Energy Report 2008) due to mostly government incentives. In 2009, the nation's wind plant fleet expanded by thirty nine percent to bring the total wind power generating capacity in the United States to over 35,000 Megawatts (MW)*. The growth in wind energy, along with gas, accounts for eighty percent of the new electricity generated in America*.

                    *American Wind Energy Association (AWEA) Q4 report 2009

According to the US Department of Energy, all US electrical energy needs could be met by the wind in Texas and the Dakotas alone. Many people are excited about wind energy, but they do not want it in their back yard. Many municipalities have passed ordinances restricting wind generators in their municipalities because they are unsightly. Hence, a national "Smart Energy Grid" is another part of the infrastructure cost to distribute wind energy efficiency (we will explore the Smart Energy Grid in detail later in this chapter).

America currently has around 52,000 Megawatts (MW) (2008 Electricity Net Generation From Renewable Energy by Energy Use Sector and Energy Source U.S. EIA) of Wind Turbines in use and around 3,000 MW in construction. From chapter one we learned wind only supplies one half of one percent of the total energy consumption in America.

Analysis:

The current price per commercial Megawatts (MW) is $1.75 Million (www.windustry.org).

To eliminate hostile foreign oil – displacing twelve percent of the US energy we need to create 744,000 MW:

$1.75Million/MW x 744,000MW = $1.3 Trillion Investment

To eliminate all foreign oil – displacing twenty-two percent of US energy we need to create 1,364,000 MW:

$1.75Million/MW x 1,364,000MW = $2.4 Trillion Investment.

The return on investment for a wind turbine varies according to the unit and location for capturing wind. According to the DOE charts, payback can vary on commercial applications from seven to sixteen years (www.windpoweringamerica.gov). Wind is a great, clean solution, but the infrastructure is too expensive for immediate substantial impact. The other problem is where to place wind farms since our communities do not want them in their back yards. The infrastructure to harness the wind in the Midwest and to distribute it around the country is not yet in place. The costs for implementing wind to help our economy and shed oil dependence are not practical for a country on a budget.

Cost for Solar

Solar "energy" encompasses three main areas: Photovoltaic, Solar Thermal, and Solar Thermal Electric. We will only examine photovoltaic (PV) in this section. This system collects solar radiation and converts it to electricity.

Since solar is relatively expensive, the number of photovoltaic systems installed in the US has been growing in recent years primarily driven by government incentives. Outside of incentives, it is hard to justify the current market costs and payback for solar photovoltaic.

Sales of solar PV modules are increasing as their efficiency increases and prices fall. A solar PV module capturing one kilowatt per square yard in peak sunlight and converting it to electricity is still relatively inefficient.

The yield would typically be 10% to 20% (for more costly units). Cost reductions for photovoltaic systems are necessary to keep this energy sector viable outside of government and/or utility incentives.

Photovoltaic trends:

+ Capacity of photovoltaic (PV) installations completed in 2008 grew by sixty three percent compared with installations in 2007, and the average size of PV systems is increasing.
+ Installation growth by capacity was largest in the nonresidential sector, but the residential sector continues to dominate the number of installations.
+ Installations in California, the dominant U.S. market, increased by ninety-five percent in 2008.

Interstate Renewable Energy Council July 09 Report

America currently has around 843 MW (**2008 Electricity Net Generation From Renewable Energy by Energy Use Sector and Energy Source U.S. EIA**) of Solar PV in use. Even with all the above stated momentum, the contribution to America's energy demand from Solar PV is only at seven tenths of one percent (.07%).

Analysis:

The national average of turnkey installed solar has declined to $7.5 Million per MW in 2008 (**The Installed Cost of Photovoltaics in the U.S. from 1998-2008: Lawrence Berkeley National Laboratory**).

To eliminate hostile foreign oil – displacing twelve percent of US energy we need to create 744,000 MW:

$7.5Million/MW x 744,000MW = $5.6 Trillion Investment

To eliminate all foreign oil – displacing twenty-two percent of US energy we need to create 1,364,000 MW:

$7.5Million /MW x 1,364,000MW = $10.2 Trillion Investment

The return on investment for a solar PV varies according to the cost of the unit, amount of sun, and local electricity rates (costs you are offsetting). According to industry graphs, the payback can be anywhere from twelve to forty years (www.solarbuzz.com). Solar has tremendous potential to be a great contributor toward energy independence for our nation. Unfortunately, the costs of the infrastructure and the inefficiency of the system can not stand alone in the market without government subsidies. At this time, solar PV is not a viable solution for renewable energy.

Cost for Biomass

Biomass Energy is produced by burning organic material as a fuel source. Some of the most popular of these renewable fuels are farm waste, crops and wood by-products.

America has the ability to produce 1.3 billion dry tons of fuel annually with very slight modifications to land use and agricultural and forestry practices (**USDA and USDOE report on Biomass as Feedstock for a Bioenergy and Bioproducts Industry**). It takes about one dry ton of biomass to produce one MW of electricity using a conventional boiler and turbine generator (**Advanced Combustion: Cofiring Coal and Biomass or Non-Recyclable Waste - Jim McMahon 2007**). Therefore, if America produces its potential in biomass fuels, we would cap out at 1.3 billion MW annually which would reduce our dependency on fossil fuels by twenty percent.

America is currently using around 55,875 MW of Biomass Energy (**2008 Electricity Net Generation From Renewable Energy by Energy Use Sector and Energy Source U.S. EIA**). Biomass accounts for 1.3% of the total energy used in America per year.

Analysis:

Because of the variety of feedstocks and processes, costs for the infrastructure and bio-power vary widely. A dedicated biomass power plant costs between $1.5 Million and $3 Million per MW (**Biomass for Power Generation and CHP – by IEA**). In the calculations below, we will use an average of $2.25 Million per MW for Biomass Energy.

To eliminate hostile foreign oil – displacing twelve percent of the US energy we need to create 744,000 MW:

$2.25Million/MW x 744,000MW = $1.7 Trillion Investment

To eliminate all foreign oil – displacing twenty-two percent of US energy we need to create 1,364,000 MW:

$2.25Million /MW x 1,364,000MW = $3.1 Trillion Investment

Biomass if over developed, can lead to competition with feedstock, food and other fiber plant production. Good farmland is not as plentiful considering the increasing demand for food from the world population. Costs are also a "Barrier to Market" considering fuel availability, transportation, and conversion efficiency. The cost per ton of biomass and non-recyclables is higher than coal. Additionally, with the cap of Biomass production, and the costs for implementation, Biomass is not a sustainable solution to the energy needs of America.

Hydropower

The first commercial hydroelectric power plant was built in 1882 on the Fox River in Appleton, Wisconsin. Now it accounts for about three percent of America's energy and is the largest contributor of renewable energy in the country. There are many advantages for hydropower.

Electricity can be produced on demand and at a constant rate (as opposed to wind and sun). Hydropower is also inexpensive after the initial cost of the facilities and dam.

Disadvantages are:
* Very expensive to build – over engineered now because of breaching concerns
* Long period for payback because of large construction costs
* Possible geological damage (example: Hoover Dam triggered a number of earthquakes)
* Environmental concerns of impacts to downstream areas and flooded areas

"Only 2,400 of the 80,000 dams in the United States are used for hydroelectric power. It is costly to construct a new hydroelectric power plant and construction uses much water and land. In addition, environmental concerns have been voiced against their use. According to the US Geological Survey, the likely trend for the future is toward small-scale hydroelectric power plants that can generate electricity for single communities."

www.waterencyclopedia.com

In summary, it looks like the US is leaving this energy sector alone because of the costs and potential environmental impacts. This is a stagnant energy sector.

Cost for Nuclear

Nuclear power is not really considered "Green Energy," but it is a source of alternative energy to fossil fuels. Environmentalists are not satisfied with the entire life cycle of the nuclear energy process. Mining uranium ore, refining and enriching the fuel, and then managing waste are usually ignored by the pro-nuclear crowd. There are a lot of processes outside the nuclear reactor that use energy and can cause environmental concern.

The United States has around sixty-five nuclear power plants (many plants have more than one reactor) in operation at this time yielding eight and one half percent of our national energy requirements.

Analysis:

To build a nuclear power plant with two cooling towers costs a minimum of ten billion dollars. The Florida Public Service Commission gives the price for two units totaling 2,200 Megawatts between twelve and eighteen billion dollars. Let's use twelve billion dollars per 2,200MW (equals $5.5 million per MW) for our analysis.

To eliminate hostile foreign oil – displacing twelve percent of the US energy we need to create 744,000 MW:

$5.5Million/MW x 744,000MW = $4.1 Trillion Investment

To eliminate all foreign oil – displacing twenty-two percent of US energy we need to create 1,364,000 MW:

$5.5Million /MW x 1,364,000MW = $7.5 Trillion Investment

The real cost/payback of nuclear power is very difficult to determine. First, all the current nuclear facilities were developed by regulated monopolies or state-owned utilities, so the numbers might not tell the entire story. The extreme costs to build these facilities are never contained and can escalate according to construction overages and resource constraints. Construction is never a fixed price, so the consumers are ultimately on the hook to pay for construction, operating expenses, and fuels no matter what the costs.

A nuclear power plant's high cost of capital for its facility, but low fuel costs leaves a lot of room for discussion on payback. Depending on the quality of the fuel, the full payback can vary from ten to eighteen years. The design life of a nuclear facility is thirty to forty years. So after the overhead of construction is paid, the variable costs for fuels and waste storage are relatively very inexpensive. However, the price tag to implement nuclear energy is extremely expensive and has many environmentalists worried about waste management of the fuel. Nuclear, therfore, is not an optimal solution, however, to eliminate foreign energy dependence and boost the economy.

National Smart Power Grid

Many of the above energy options assume we can distribute energy across America on a national "Smart Energy Grid." This grid has not been erected yet, and we might not even really understand how to build one. The alternative is to have wind, solar and/or nuclear power plants distributed across the country to more efficiently distribute electricity without large voltage drops.

> "To bring transmission and wind generation together on a national scale... is a theoretical interstate 765 kV electricity transportation system that encompasses major portions of the United States connecting areas of high wind resource potential with major load centers. It is projected that an interstate EHV (Extra High Voltage to reduce voltage drops) transmission system could enable significantly greater wind energy penetration levels by providing an additional 200-400 GW of bulk transmission capacity. The total capital investment is estimated at approximately $60 billion (2007 dollars). While it is by no means the total solution, this initiative illustrates the opportunities that exist..."
> **American Electric Power Interstate Transmission Vision for Wind Integration**

Sixty billion dollars is not the full picture to build a complete "Smart Grid." There is not a firm number as to how to complete the project or how much it would cost.

Conservation

Converting to renewable energy is expensive and not the cure for a nation that has a weak economy. Conservation of energy to stretch our resources is a practical measure we do as individuals to save money. The government has joined in to help us save resources by giving incentives for energy saving practices. Not to be too obvious, but we can not imagine how much it costs in taxes to have the government create and monitor these "Incentives" for us to save money on *our* energy. Why not cut our taxes in general and let the free market take its course with supply and demand? That would help improve the economy. This would eliminate some government overhead, improve the economy, and still reap the results of energy savings.

The following are areas of conservation:
+ Tax breaks on efficient energy star appliances
+ Tax breaks on efficient HVAC
+ Tax breaks on sealing homes
+ Tax breaks on efficient cars
+ Tax breaks on solar products
+ Cash for Clunkers car program (Tried for a while in 2009)
+ Increasing energy efficient standards for construction

Do not misunderstand; efficiency investments are permanent tasks that are important implementations for cost savings. Once efficiency measures are implemented, they are not undone when energy costs decrease. Conservation investments are much more important than small behavioral changes that are temporary reactions to spikes in energy costs (i.e. reducing driving because of high fuel costs).

However, these are good and reasonable actions. People will alter their plans and lifestyles for a return on their investment and to save money on energy costs over time - a free market experience. Personally, we believe the American people are smart enough to understand saving money.

The real issue is not the lack of resources, as we are led to believe, but tapping into our resources to prosper again. You cannot starve yourself out of hunger; you have to find food to stay healthy. We need to feed our national economy- not starve it more.

Summary

It is clear the capital investment to move away from foreign oil dependence only to renewable energy will be expensive. The incentives for an affordable renewable energy transition will be accounted for later in this book. Special interest groups are pushing to migrate only to renewable energy at the expense of the taxpayers. The idea of immediately converting America's energy source to a more expensive renewable infrastructure is just not practical. At this time, our country simply cannot afford to go deeper in debt over energy. The point is to work with business through a planned logical recovery process so America can prosper. Government does not contribute to the Gross National Product - business does.

Our intent is not to present a solution to displace fossil fuels with renewable energy. There are many combinations, theories, discussions and presentations about the best way to migrate to renewable energy from fossil fuels, but the cost benefits are not there yet. We will present a solution to our current energy dependence on foreign oil supplies which will enable us to stop sending over three hundred billion dollars overseas to other economies and effectively draining our economic wealth.

Sweden has the most formal aggressive goal to eliminate foreign energy dependence by 2020. Sweden relies on fossil fuels primarily for transportation and gets most of its electricity from hydroelectric power and nuclear power. Geothermal energy and waste generate most of the heating requirements for the nation. We are a little behind Sweden, but if we work through a transition period to get our economy strong, we can aggressively pursue cheaper alternative energy solutions and fund new technologies.

Just a side note: The pursuit for energy independence does not have to take generations. Lamp oil from whales lit most American homes in 1850, but in the next nine years, almost all the whale oil market turned to **less expensive** and smarter solutions. Imagine that - the government did not have to interfere, and free enterprise worked it all out back then...

CHAPTER 3

Environmentalist or Imperialists?

As long as the earth endures, seedtime and harvest, cold and heat, summer and winter, day and night will never cease.

Genesis 8:22 (NIV)

There are many pure environmentalists who are sincerely concerned with preserving the environment with no outside agenda. We are a part of this group. In almost any established movement, a "fanatical" sect evolves that pushes another more self-serving agenda. It is really easy to find the people who are exploiting the environmental cause - just follow the money and their emotional (not scientific) platforms. Please bear with us concerning this sensitive subject as we have collected only a handful of facts to present our case. We have included this topic in the book because some "Environmentalist" opinions are hindering the nation's economic progress.

In this chapter we are going to look at:
+ Global Warming History
+ Scientific Letter of Skepticism
+ Data and Analysis

- Climate-Gate
- The CO2 Issue
- Hidden Agendas

The Global Warming and "Cap and Trade" movements have worked our country and most parts of the world into a frenzy. Global Warming and Cap and Trade have evolved into a religion for those who have bought into its theology. Since the premise of these movements have very loose scientific facts, the leaders have turned to the media and have appealed to the emotional side of a deteriorating world based on industrialism. Hence, creating the impression that anything involving fossil fuels would only put another nail in the coffin of our children's environment. Let's analyze these sensational appeals and why they are being made.

Global Warming History

Roger Revelle was a notable research scientist in San Diego. He studied and released a research paper on the effects of burning fossil fuels and the greenhouse effect this caused in the atmosphere. His report was the trigger that gave the United Nations Intergovernmental Panel on Climate Change the ammunition they needed to start the global warming movement. This same Roger Revelle became the professor of Al Gore at Harvard. Although Mr. Revelle reported before his death in 1991 that his theory on global warming was wrong, Mr. Gore refused to listen to his professor and even proclaimed the professor was senile. The Global Warming movement was underway, and those who opposed it were identified as scientific heretics and evil capitalists.

When Al Gore left politics, he was worth around two million dollars; now his worth is estimated at over *a hundred million dollars* from movies, speaking engagements, and Nobel prizes. Wealth amassed in the name of saving the planet from Global Warming and pushing the "Cap and Trade" agenda. As soon as financial grants started being given out, every

26

scientist and researcher with a thermometer began to cry global warming or climate change to keep the money flowing from the foundations. There are large sums of money riding on Global Warming.

Who will benefit from these climate change theories that CO2 causes the earth to heat up (the premise behind Cap and Trade) to a point that it causes world catastrophes? The benefactors are the lobbyists who are paid by environmental groups, the shell companies that are established to promote green technologies, and industries monitoring CO2. For example, Al Gore sits on the board of a company called Hara. Hara stands to profit **billions of dollars** monitoring companies who will be forced to adhere to costly CO2 regulations that are proven not be a threat to the environment.

Al Gore and Global Warming "Scientists" have continuously refused to debate any informed scientist about Global Warming. Instead they use the media to "Market" their agenda. The Global Warming movement has added to the sensational appeal that has misled our country into thinking we are at the last junction of saving our planet. They want us to discontinue using fossil fuels immediately and reinvent industry to save the earth. It is easy to be swept away by the climate change movement from media reporting. Most people who believe in Global Warming are following what they perceive as the right thing to do for our earth, nation and future generations. The following arguments are critical in understanding that we can supply our own energy which will produce an energy independent country having a healthy economy.

Scientific Letter of Skepticism

This letter addressed to the United Nations Secretary-General, Ban Ki Moon, from 141 prominent scientists states that the verdict behind anthropogenic global warming is anything but proven. These scientists have no agenda but to inform the public of scientific evidence. Following is a copy of the letter:

"His Excellency Ban Ki Moon
Secretary-General, United Nations
New York, NY
United States of America

8 December 2009

Dear Secretary-General,

Climate change science is in a period of 'negative discovery' - the more we learn about this exceptionally complex and rapidly evolving field the more we realize how little we know. Truly, the science is NOT settled.

Therefore, there is no sound reason to impose expensive and restrictive public policy decisions on the peoples of the Earth without first providing convincing evidence that human activities are causing dangerous climate change beyond that resulting from natural causes. Before any precipitate action is taken, we must have solid observational data demonstrating that recent changes in climate differ substantially from changes observed in the past and are well in excess of normal variations caused by solar cycles, ocean currents, changes in the Earth's orbital parameters and other natural phenomena.

We the undersigned, being qualified in climate-related scientific disciplines, challenge the UNFCCC and supporters of the United Nations Climate Change Conference to produce convincing OBSERVATIONAL EVIDENCE for their claims of dangerous human-caused global warming and other changes in climate. Projections of possible future scenarios from unproven computer models of climate are not acceptable substitutes for real world data obtained through unbiased and rigorous scientific investigation.

Specifically, we challenge supporters of the hypothesis of dangerous human-caused climate change to demonstrate that:

1. Variations in global climate in the last hundred years are significantly outside the natural range experienced in previous centuries;
2. Humanity's emissions of carbon dioxide and other 'greenhouse gases' (GHG) are having a dangerous impact on global climate;
3. Computer-based models can meaningfully replicate the impact of all of the natural factors that may significantly influence climate;
4. Sea levels are rising dangerously at a rate that has accelerated with increasing human GHG emissions, thereby threatening small islands and coastal communities;
5. The incidence of malaria is increasing due to recent climate changes;
6. Human society and natural ecosystems cannot adapt to foreseeable climate change as they have done in the past;
7. Worldwide glacier retreat, and sea ice melting in Polar Regions, is unusual and related to increases in human GHG emissions;
8. Polar bears and other Arctic and Antarctic wildlife are unable to adapt to anticipated local climate change effects, independent of the causes of those changes;
9. Hurricanes, other tropical cyclones and associated extreme weather events are increasing in severity and frequency;
10. Data recorded by ground-based stations are a reliable indicator of surface temperature trends.

It is not the responsibility of 'climate realist' scientists to prove that dangerous human-caused climate change is not happening. Rather, it is those who propose that it is, and promote the allocation of massive investments to solve the supposed 'problem', who have the obligation to convincingly demonstrate that recent climate change is not of mostly natural origin and, if we do nothing, catastrophic change will ensue. To date, this they have utterly failed to do so."

Signed by 141 Top Scientists from around the world including:

1. Habibullo I. Abdussamatov, Dr. Sci., mathematician and astrophysicist, Head of the Russian-Ukrainian Astrometria project on the board of the Russian segment of the ISS, Head of Space Research Laboratory at the Pulkovo Observatory of the Russian Academy of Sciences, St. Petersburg, Russia

2. Göran Ahlgren, docent organisk kemi, general secretary of the Stockholm Initiative, Professor of Organic Chemistry, Stockholm, Sweden

3. Syun-Ichi Akasofu, PhD, Professor of Physics, Emeritus and Founding Director, International Arctic Research Center of the University of Alaska, Fairbanks, Alaska, U.S.A.

4. J.R. Alexander, Professor Emeritus, Dept. of Civil Engineering, University of Pretoria, South Africa; Member, UN Scientific and Technical Committee on Natural Disasters, 1994-2000, Pretoria, South Africa.

5. Jock Allison, PhD, ONZM, formerly Ministry of Agriculture Regional Research Director, Dunedin, New Zealand

6. Bjarne Andresen, PhD, Dr. Science, Physicist, published and presents on the impossibility of a "global temperature", Professor, The Niels Bohr Institute, University of Copenhagen, Denmark

7. Timothy F. Ball, PhD, environmental consultant and former climatology professor, University of Winnipeg, Member, Science Advisory Board, ICSC, Victoria, British Columbia, Canada

8. Douglas W. Barr, BS (Meteorology, University of Chicago), BS and MS (Civil Engineering, University of Minnesota), Barr Engineering Co. (environmental issues and water resources), Minnesota, U.S.A.

9. Romuald Bartnik, PhD (Organic Chemistry), Professor Emeritus, Former chairman of the Department of Organic

and Applied Chemistry, climate work in cooperation with Department of Hydrology and Geological Museum, University of Lodz, Lodz, Poland

10. Colin Barton, B.Sc., PhD, Earth Science, Principal research scientist (retd), Commonwealth Scientific and Industrial Research Organisation (CSIRO), Melbourne, Victoria, Australia

Data and Analysis

There are numerous scientific studies that prove the earth is not warming but actually might be doing the opposite – *cooling*. Following is just one of the many studies conducted:

The following data has been reported by the National Snow and Ice Data Center at the University of Colorado. Since measurements began in 1979, the Antarctic sea ice has expanded, contrary to what the alarmists and news media are reporting:

	Extent	Concentration
2009	16.3 million sq km	11.6 million sq km
1995	16.0 million sq km	11.4 million sq km
1979	15.9 million sq km	11.2 million sq km

According to NOAA GISS data winter temperatures in the Antarctic have actually fallen by 1°F since 1957, with the coldest year being 2004.

This data does not help the Global Warming cause. This is not an anti-Global Warming book, so our intent is not to overwhelm you with lots of statistics. Please do the research, and you will be convinced the climate change movement does not have legitimate facts to support it. There is an abundance of scientific evidence to discredit this huge movement.

"Climate-Gate"

If you have not heard of "Climate Gate," it is because the media did not give it sufficient coverage. Following is a commentary explaining how leading "scientists" have tried to cover their position for such a long time. The cat came out of the bag when these emails leaked and exposed the climate change research team. Even with such shocking news, the press was lacking in coverage of this debacle.

"Last week, someone (probably a whistle-blower at the Climate Research Unit at the University of East Anglia, England) released e-mails and other documents written by Phil Jones, Michael Mann and other leading "scientists" who edit and control the content of the reports of the Intergovernmental Panel on Climate Change. The e-mails appear to show a conspiracy to falsify data and suppress academic debate in order to exaggerate the possible threat of man-made global warming.

The misconduct exposed by the e-mails is so apparent that one scientist, Tim Ball, said it marked "the death blow to climate science." Another, Patrick Michaels, told the New York Times: "This is not a smoking gun; this is a mushroom cloud." ...

The implications of these e-mails are enormous: They mean the IPCC is not a reliable source of science on global warming.

And since the global movement to "do something" about global warming rests almost entirely on the IPCC's claim to represent the "consensus" of climate science, that entire movement stands discredited.

The release of these documents creates an opportunity for reporters, academics, politicians and others who relied on the IPCC to form their opinion about global warming to stop and reconsider their position.

The experts they trusted and quoted in the past have been caught red-handed plotting to conceal data, hide temperature trends that contradict their predictions and keep critics from appearing in peer-reviewed journals. This is real evidence they should examine and then comment on publicly."

Joseph Bast, 'Climate-Gate' Scandal Should Be
Wake-Up Call For Press, Politicians

We could not have said it better. If you have any other doubts, please research this for yourself and do not follow sensationalism from the media, but verify sources. Right from the source itself, the climate change "scientists" confirmed this is one of the largest scams the "scientific community" has ever participated in.

The CO2 Issue

Cap and Trade legislation to limit Carbon Dioxide (CO2) emissions is being negotiated through the government as this book is being written. Cap and Trade is a tax on energy to level the costs of renewable energy with the cost of fossil fuels. The large utilities emitting CO2 (which is natural and used by plants for photosynthesis) will have a cap on their emissions and will have to purchase ("Trade" for) renewable energy credits from utilities who are not emitting their quota of CO2. For example, a coal burning plant will have to purchase "Carbon Credits" from a wind plant (who does not burn) which helps offset the cost of wind. The result of this program will be utilities increasing their rates to cover for purchasing carbon credits (essentially like another tax).

There is absolutely no proof that the Cap and Trade "Tax" will improve the environment for humans or the earth. Scientists have actually stated that if the Cap and Trade legislation passes, it will not impact the environment at all. In essence, the government would be instituting more regulations hampering our economy. Proponents of Cap and Trade argue that man has created a tremendous amount of CO2 since the industrial revolution. They believe we have turned the balance of carbon into overload. It makes logical sense, but actually, quite the opposite is true. Please note Dr. Wolfgang Knorr's research:

"New data show that the balance between the airborne and the absorbed fraction of carbon dioxide has stayed approximately constant since 1850, despite emissions of carbon dioxide having risen from about 2 billion tons a year in 1850 to 35 billion tons a year now.

This suggests that terrestrial ecosystems and the oceans have a much greater capacity to absorb CO2 than had been previously expected. The results run contrary to a significant body of recent research which expects that the capacity of terrestrial ecosystems and the oceans to absorb CO2 should start to diminish as CO2 emissions increase, letting greenhouse gas levels skyrocket. Dr Wolfgang Knorr at the University of Bristol found that in fact the trend in the airborne fraction since 1850 has only been 0.7 ± 1.4% per decade, which is essentially zero."

University of Bristol - Controversial new climate change results Press release issued 9 November 2009

Carbon, which drives many environmental activists, is really not an issue as defined by science. Cap and Trade proponents are categorizing carbon the same way they categorized sulfur when its pollution created acid rain – not the same animal. We are not supporting irresponsible actions toward the environment, but we have to act on movements that make sense and not waste time and money. Fossil fuels are not contributing to the demise of the earth as we know it.

Hidden Agendas

Is there another movement growing on the world stage and hiding under the guise of Carbon and Global Warming? Please analyze the following:

> From the Copenhagen summit:
> "The pact calls on developed nations to provide $30 billion to help developing nations deal with the effects of climate change from 2010 to 2012. By 2020, the text says rich nations "set a goal of mobilizing jointly $100 billion a year" for poor nations." –
> **The Wall Street Journal**

There have been numerous sources showing that the climate change data has been manipulated to produce the results desired by the **Intergovernmental Panel on Climate Change** (IPCC) which is employed by the United Nations (UN). If the panel can produce results showing the world's climate is changing because of the actions of advanced countries, then those industrious countries can be "penalized" for their actions and their wealth can be redistributed to underdeveloped countries. So along comes Al Gore who gives credence to the idea that Global Warming is a threat to our environment and is warmly received by Dr. Rajendra Pachauri, head of the IPCC. Dr. Pachauri is completely supported by the UN because climate change is the best option for world cooperation to reel in funds and power for the UN. In the meantime, our Congress gives credence to this movement, our country goes farther in debt and our economy continues to suffer.

The goal of the United Nations is to patrol and control this "environmental fund" acting as a New World Government! Why else would the UN be so eager to back Global Warming and not approach it scientifically? The IPCC and other "environmental" groups are pursuing power to establish a redistribution of wealth in the world. The United States would be foolish to follow this "tax on industry" when most of the rising economies around the world are ignoring it. China and India's economies are growing extremely fast making the global market place very competitive. By adopting another erroneous tax on industry, the United States will be hamstrung in the global marketplace.

The world needs to understand there is a massive effort to set up a world governing body. It is based on the belief that unifying the world will save humanity from pending ecological disaster. Nothing could be farther from the truth. After the fall of communism and the defeat of fascism, these ideologues did not just die out. Environmental movements are a new host for these spirits to occupy in order to stay alive and push their agendas. It would be the biggest coup if the fascists, communists and socialists that have been deemed dead rise up under this new banner and create their "One World Government." The United States and other countries need to stay vigilant and always search for the truth.

Logistically, the world cannot afford to shift its balance of agricultural production to follow the incentives for Cap and Trade on the basis of climate change. This world movement could actually affect food production because there would be more farmers producing bio diesel instead of food products. The result could cause over one billion people to suffer from hunger due to increasing food prices.

Vaclay Klaus knows communism first hand since he grew up under an occupied Czech Republic by the Soviet Union. He is adamantly against this environmental movement and speaks out strongly in his new book:

> "The environmentalists' attitude toward nature is analogous to the Marxist approach to economics. The aim in both cases is to replace the free, spontaneous evolution of the world (and humankind) by the would-be optimal, central or-using today's fashionable adjective-global planning of world development. Much as in the case of Communism, this approach is utopian and would lead to results completely different from the intended ones. Like other utopias,

this one can never materialize, and efforts to make it materialize can only be carried out through restrictions of freedom, through the dictates of a small, elitist minority over the overwhelming majority. In the past 150 years (at least since Marx), the socialists have been very effectively destroying human freedom under humane and compassionate slogans, such as caring for man, ensuring social equality, and fostering social welfare. The environmentalists are doing the same under equally noble-minded slogans, expressing concern about nature more than about people (recall their radical motto 'Earth first'). In both cases, the slogans have been (and still are) just a smokescreen. In both cases, the movements were (and are) completely about power, about the hegemony of the 'chosen ones' (as they see themselves) over the rest of us, about the imposition of the only correct worldview (their own), about the remodeling of the world."

Environmentalism is the new communism, a system of elite command-and-control that kills prosperity and should similarly be condemned to the ash heap of history"

Quoted from "Blue Planet in Green Shackles"
by Czech President Vaclay Klaus

The goal of the United Nations is to control the wealth of the United States and other industrialized countries who will listen to its arguments. This wealth will be redistributed among the other nations of the world to level a lopsided playing field caused by our ingenuity and efforts. Our country is the brightest, most creative, futuristic nation on earth, and we have been blessed by God. This positioning of our nation has created international envy by those nations who want what we have with a belief they are "entitled" to our wealth.

Summary:

There are many productive environmental movements that are created to solve real issues such as deforestation, over-fishing, pollution, clean water, waste management, pesticide management, etc. Global Warming and

Cap and Trade are not real issues but contrived for furthering personal agendas. Actually, it is extremely sad that the world has spent so much time and money on these "environmental issues" when there are very real issues out there that are not getting any attention. Our country cannot afford to follow these expensive and economically crippling agendas.

It is interesting that Global Warming and the CO2 effort has drawn from both sides of the spectrum: extreme capitalists who are producing as much wealth as possible and the imperialists who believe government should have total control over your freedoms. Both of these motivations need to be seen for what they are - impediments preventing any progress for the United States to become energy independent. Fossil fuels are not the demons that are jeopardizing our existence on this earth, but these "Environmentalists" might be...

CHAPTER 4

The US National Debt

Nothing is so well calculated to produce a death-like torpor in the country as an extended system of taxation and a great national debt.

William Cobbett, letter, Feb. 10, 1804

Why in the world are we now talking about the national debt in a book on energy and solutions? The US National Debt is so large that it is a factor in our economy and our nation's security. This animal has to be addressed sooner than later or America will follow the paths of countries like Greece.

In this Chapter we will look at:
+ History of the National Debt
+ The True Debt
+ Who Owns the National Debt
+ Impact of Debt On Economy

The debt is real and will not be going away without focusing our attention on it. Since the US National Debt is a very important part of the solution, we need to understand it.

History

Let's go back in America's history to understand how we created the vehicle, systems, and procedures to be able to legally accumulate such massive debt.

Alexander Hamilton, the first Secretary of the Treasury, persuaded the Founding Fathers to form a Central Banking System that would allow the newly formed government to borrow money when necessary. This is the same model the British Government operated under to borrow money primarily during times of war when reserve funds were necessary. This argument was well received by most of the Founding Fathers because the newly formed country was low in liquid available cash.

Once the Central Banking System was instituted, the new government was secure financially in case of wars and/or other major capital improvement projects. The problem, as shown in the chart below, is America keeps on spending and does not take responsibility to reduce principle. Please note the major trends in debt additions throughout America's history:

Year	Debt Amount	Comments
1791	$75,463,476.52	First Fiscal Year for US
1812	$45,209,737.90	War of 1812- US 1st war
1816	$127,334,933.74	War of 1812 Debt Accumulation
1835	$33,733.05	Note how the debt was worked down
1857	$28,699,831.85	Benchmark before the Civil War
1866	$2,773,236,173.69	Civil War Debt Accumulation
1890	$1,552,140,204.73	Gov't Working Down the Civil War Debt
1916	$3,609,244,262.16	Benchmark before WWI
1919	$27,390,970,113.12	WWI Debt Accumulation
1931	$16,801,281,491.71	Working Through the Great Depression
1940	$42,967,531,037.68	Benchmark Before WWII
1946	$269,422,099,173.26	WWII Debt Accumulation
1950	$257,357,352,351.04	Note: Debt has not been paid down since
1960	$286,330,760,848.37	
1970	$370,918,706,949.93	
1975	$533,189,000,000.00	

1980	$907,701,000,000.00
1985	$1,823,103,000,000.00
1990	$3,233,313,451,777.25
1995	$4,973,982,900,709.39
2000	$5,674,178,209,886.86
2005	$7,932,709,661,723.50
2008	$10,024,724,896,912.49
2010	$12,578,000,000,000.00 And Counting

Source: U.S. Department of the Treasury Bureau

The National Debt is close to *Thirteen Trillion dollars* at the time of this writing (Spring 2010). The debt is an accumulation of budget deficits - simply put, overspending by the government. Since 1950, the US Government has not applied *any* money toward reducing the National Debt's principle.

America, as well as any entity in business or public service, operating with a huge escalating deficit for over sixty years is raising current and potential future investor's concerns. Historically, the US has had a very strong and stable economy and has proven to pay the interest payments on its debt. As the National Debt approaches the Gross National Product (GNP) the concerns for lending and stability of our government becomes questionable. Once our government becomes a concern, the holders of the debt demand larger interest payments to compensate for the perceived increased risk of not being repaid. Eventually, the increasing percentage of interest plus the already massive debt, will only suppress our government and economy to force the debt to stay within a reasonable limit. In other words, if the debt is not attractive, no one will be purchasing it and our country's economy will suffer tremendously.

In the business world, it would be impossible to operate and stay in business by continuously borrowing to stay afloat. It is quite ironic that the government of "Free Enterprise" does not understand and/or operate under the same basic principles of its own economy. The debt is getting so large that it has to be addressed, or it will stifle America's economy for many generations - if not strangle the economy altogether.

One of the main responsibilities of our government is to protect our wealth and let the citizens prosper under our free enterprise economic system. It is quite ironic that most of our representatives in government *never* owned or operated a business. It is also ironic that not one person in the current administration's inner circle has owned a traditional business, yet they wonder why the economy is suffering. Our government needs to be educated in how a free enterprise economy actually works in order to operate by the same rules.

From a political point of view, the economy and voters benefit from deficit spending for a short period of time. The politicians implement and continue "feel good" spending to give the opinion they are benefiting America, its voters, and/or lobbyists. The difficult and unpopular task for politicians is to cut spending and government programs because voters do not want government perks taken away.

Just a plug for term limits here: we would probably not be in this situation if we had term limits for government representatives. Career politicians will do whatever they can to stay in power even if it jeopardizes generations to come. With term limits, representatives are more likely to act in a responsible way and address the hard issues today when not worried about reelection. We will hit this again later.

Now is the time to address the national debt seriously. We have heard politicians for the last sixty years talk about it, but the numbers prove in the chart above that no action has been taken by our politicians to reduce the national debt - just political promises.

The True Debt

As stated before, at the time of this writing the US National Debt is right at *thirteen trillion dollars* and increasing at a rate of almost *four billion dollars* a day. The US has the highest national debt in the world. The reported national debt amount is published by the US Government, which should make us a little suspicious. There are future financial responsibilities the government has not included in this reporting. These obligations include borrowing from other US government departments.

Following are US Government investment funds. Each fund has over *one hundred billion* dollars invested in the national debt:

- Civil Service Retirement Fund
- Department of Defense Military Retirement Fund
- Department of Defense, Medicare Eligible Retiree Fund
- Federal Disability Insurance Trust Fund
- Federal Hospital Insurance Trust Fund
- Federal Old Age and Survivors Insurance Trust Fund
- Federal Supplementary Medical Insurance Trust Fund

Note: There are more than 70 other "smaller" investment funds from the Government besides the ones listed above.

U.S. Department of the Treasury Bureau – Summary of Treasury Securities Outstanding

The real national debt for future obligations including borrowing from Government programs, is closer to *fifty-five trillion dollars.*

Here is the breakdown of the government's total obligations:

$12 Trillion – Reported National Debt Fall 2009
$36 Trillion – Medicare Future Obligations
$6.6 Trillion – S. Security & other Gov't Retirement Obligations
$55 Trillion - Total (some say this figure is around $70+ Trillion)

Source: 2008 Financial Report of the United States Government

The government has the obligation to fufill Medicare's three programs: hospital insurance, outpatient, and prescription drugs. The current and future promised Medicare benefits amount to *thirty-six trillion* dollars as our population ages. The government can, however, change its amount of coverage to increase or decrease the value of benefits. It would be difficult for politicians to cut back benefits to save on its obligations. So, the government would probably have to increase taxes again to help cover costs. This will not help the economy.

Fifty-five trillion dollars costs each citizen, adults and children, around *one hundred eighty thousand dollars* to eliminate the real national debt. The figure for the average family is close to *five hundred thousand dollars*. This does not account for the tremendous on-going operating expenses of our government - at the city, county, state, and federal levels.

From the appearance of this debt accumulation and the future obligations of the government's contractual obligations, it looks like America is playing a most dangerous Ponzi scheme. The US Government requires a tremendous and increasing amount of borrowing to handle its obligations and avoid financial implosion. If not corrected, at some point the Ponzi scheme always ends in a catastrophe. It is kind of ironic that our court system convicted Bernard Madoff of one of the largest Ponzi schemes known, but allows our government to operate under the same principles.

Who Owns the Debt

The investors of America's national debt are categorized into three areas: US Government's Intergovernmental debt, US publicly held debt, and foreign publicly held debt. The investment community invests in the national debt by purchasing Treasury Bills, Notes and Bonds. The breakdown of US Government intergovernmental debt using temporary surpluses from retirement funds, insurances, and public health funds was reviewed in the previous section.

The United States' publicly held debt is purchased by US individuals and corporations that are US based. These entities have traditionally invested into government-backed debt because of its security and guaranteed interest returns.

The foreign publicly held debt is a concern because the US government has to deal with the international community and maintain its good relations with countries who own our debt. Any party investing in an entity will always have an influence on that entity. With the current US government financial situation, we cannot afford to negatively impact relations with countries investing in our debt (i.e.: play hardball with China concerning unfair trade practices). Since our debt is always increasing, our government knows it will need more capital from these foreign sources to operate. The following statistics show the percentage of national debt owned by foreign countries as of July 2009 (keep in mind foreign debt is 28% of America's total national debt):

Country	% of Foreign Debt	% of Total US Debt
People's Republic of China	23.35%	6.54%
Japan	21.13%	5.93%
United Kingdom	6.42%	1.80%
Caribbean banking centers	5.64%	1.58%
Oil exporters	5.52%	1.55%
Brazil	4.03%	1.13%
Russia	3.44%	1.00%
Hong Kong	3.36%	.94%
Luxembourg	2.69%	.75%
Taiwan R.O.C.	2.26%	.63%
Switzerland	1.99%	.56%
Germany	1.64%	.46%
Singapore	1.24%	.35%
India	1.13%	.32%
Republic of Ireland	1.13%	.32%
Korea	1.10%	.31%
Thailand	0.92%	.26%

Norway	0.84%	.24%
Mexico	0.81%	.23%
Turkey	0.80%	.22%
France	0.72%	.20%
Netherlands	0.63%	.18%
Canada	0.59%	.17%
Egypt	0.54%	.15%
Italy	0.51%	.14%
Israel	0.49%	.14%
Sweden	0.48%	.13%
Belgium	0.46%	.13%
Colombia	0.43%	.12%
Chile	0.39%	.11%
Malaysia	0.35%	.10%
Philippines	0.33%	.10%
All other	4.66%	1.30%

Note: The Bureau of International Settlements suspects the primary holdings by Belgium, Caribbean Banking Centers and Luxembourg totaling 8.8%, are fronts for various oil-exporting countries or hedge funds that do not wish to be identified.

Source: U.S. Treasury Department.

Foreign countries have increased holdings from 13% in 1988 to 28% in 2009. Unless the Ponzi scheme style of operation is addressed, foreign investment will continue to grow so the US can make good on its obligations. Within the next 20 years, US-backed retirement accounts and social health care will need repayment because of the aging population. If we take the major percentage of the US Government Intragovernmental debt (retirement funds, insurances, and public health funds) out of the national debt equation, then nearly half of the US debt will have to be replaced by another entity - America will practically be on the auction block.

Impact of Debt on Economy

We have talked about various impacts on America's economy and security because of a runaway national debt. As America's debt reaches its GNP, foreign countries will start to shy away from the once secure investment in the US Government/economy. America will have to cut back on programs since it will not have the funds to support the aging population. The US Government has already started printing money thus diluting the dollar. Foreign investors will flee from this scenario of "inflation" because their net investments will be worth less than the money invested. Another risk of printing money is hyperinflation. Once a country gets caught in hyperinflation, the economy will spiral down quickly and it is very hard to remedy.

What our government is consistently good at is increasing taxes. Taxes have increased steadily throughout America's history and have produced one of the most complicated tax structures in the world (food for another book). As demonstrated over the last fifty years, increased taxes have *not* touched the principle balance of the national debt. The ramifications of higher taxes are pushing industry and wealth out of the country into international havens. North America is already witnessing many wealthy retirees leaving America to retire in more affordable countries where the dollar has more purchasing power, not as many taxes, and better services. The government is actually squeezing the wealth out of America through increased taxation.

Summary

"I place economy among the first and most important virtues, and public debt as the greatest of dangers to be feared. To preserve our independence, we must not let our rulers load us with perpetual debt. If we run into such debts, we must be taxed in our meat and drink, in our necessities and in our comforts, in our labor and in our amusements. If we can prevent the government from wasting the labor of the people, under the pretense of caring for them, they will be happy."

Thomas Jefferson

In summary, the large Federal debt will continue to strangle America's economy. We need to address this issue now and not let the national debt continue to grow. The government's Ponzi scheme financing mode of operation is not sustainable. Our nation's economy and security are at stake. We need a solution to create a strong economy, cut government spending, and pay down the national debt...

CHAPTER 5

Government Overhaul

*I think we have more machinery of government than is necessary,
too many parasites living on the labor of the industrious.*

Thomas Jefferson

*Man is not free unless government is limited. There's a clear
cause and effect here that is as neat and predictable as a law
of physics: As government expands, liberty contracts.*

Ronald Reagan

We need to analyze our government to see how effective it is in the twenty first century. Is the government protecting its citizens and giving them the freedoms to prosper, or is the government becoming a hindrance to the American people. In the business world, consultants identify opportunities for maximizing process efficiencies for their clients. Then basic steps are taken to streamline and automate processes to maximize efficiency and decrease overhead (operating expenses). Similarly, our tax dollars should be used in the most efficient manor at all government levels - not squandered.

In this Chapter we will explore:

+ Purpose of Government
+ Differing Government Views
+ Term Limits
+ Government Salaries
+ Restructuring Ideas
+ Representative Overhead
+ Who Should Vote

Purpose of Government

We hold these truths to be self-evident, that all men are created equal, that they are endowed by their Creator with certain unalienable Rights, that among these are Life, Liberty and the pursuit of Happiness. That to secure these rights, Governments are instituted among Men, deriving their just powers from the consent of the governed.

United States Declaration of Independence

John Locke, one of the most influential men in history whose works shaped our government wrote:

"Men being, as has been said, by nature all free, equal, and independent, no one can be put out of this estate and subjected to the political power of another without his own consent, which is done by agreeing with other men, to join and unite into a community for their comfortable, safe, and peaceable living, one amongst another, in a secure enjoyment of their properties, and a greater security against any that are not of it. This any number of men may do, because it injures not the freedom of the rest; they are left, as they were, in the liberty of the state of Nature. When any number of men have so consented to make one community or government, they are thereby presently incorporated, and make one body politic, wherein the majority have a right to act and conclude the rest."

An essay concerning the true original, extent and end of civil government (1690)

God created the boundaries of nature and set in motion the laws and grace of the family unit. From the very first family unit, society had its initial form of government established. Over a period of time the community that established and molded the government can begin to be suppressed by the same very government formed to protect it. Thus, the control has actually left the people and is now with the government. The government being in control creates a state of welfare for its citizens while typically, in the real world, maintains a lavish lifestyle for the governing members.

Differing Government Views

Following are the differing government views in a democracy:

Conservatives favor economic freedoms and typically support laws to restrict behavior violating traditional values. They oppose excessive government control of business, while endorsing government action to defend morality and the traditional family structure. Conservatives usually support a strong military, oppose bureaucracy and high taxes, favor a free-market economy, and endorse strong law enforcement.

Liberals support significant government control of the economy and typically embrace freedom of choice in personal matters. They generally support a government funded "safety net" to help the disadvantaged, and advocate strict regulation of business. Liberals tend to favor environmental regulations, defend civil liberties and free expression, support government action to promote equality, and tolerate diverse lifestyles.

Libertarians support maximum liberty in both personal and economic matters. They advocate a much smaller government: one that is limited to protecting individuals from coercion and violence. Libertarians tend to embrace individual responsibility, oppose government bureaucracy and taxes, promote private charity, tolerate diverse lifestyles, support the free market, and defend civil liberties.

Centrists espouse a "middle ground" regarding government control of the economy and personal behavior. Depending on the issue, they sometimes favor government intervention and sometimes support individual freedom of choice. Centrists pride themselves on keeping an open mind, tend to oppose "political extremes," and emphasize what they describe as "practical" solutions to problems.

Statists (Big Government) want government to have a great deal of power over the economy and individual behavior. They frequently doubt whether economic liberty and individual freedom are practical options in today's world. Statists tend to distrust the free market, support high taxes and centralized planning of the economy, oppose diverse lifestyles, and question the importance of civil liberties.

Socialism, communism, and all political structures outside of a true democracy are in theory wonderful semi-utopias that would work extremely well *if* human nature could be altered. Very few people will work hard for the good of the "State", but they will work extremely hard for bettering their own position in life personally and for their family. Because of the need for power ("Self Actualization") and greed, rulers in basically every race and society will bend to the temptation of pursuing selfish ambitions instead of governing for the betterment of the citizens they shepherd. Checks and balances need to be in place for government officials.

As a note: anytime a society replaces God with the "State" as seen throughout history, that government will only last as long as it can suppress its citizens. This is usually accomplished by force, lack of educating the population, and operating by use of fear. The society without God and freedom becomes a hell on earth for its population.

Our Country is letting atheists take away the power our God-fearing forefathers set as a foundation. At the birth of our Country we were truly "Under God," but now that term and "God we Trust" are barely in our anthems, pledges or on printed money. God is constantly being attacked by the society created under Him. Prayer has been taken out of school, the Ten Commandments are not permitted on Government property and God is not welcome under the guise of separation of "Church and State." Religious separation from the State does not mean religious censorship or abstinence. Without God and a higher moral law than "Uncle Sam" our Country will continue to face moral, ethical, and spiritual decay. This eventually leads to loss of freedoms as the State becomes the god. Loss of freedoms leads to loss of security, both personal and national, and economic degradation. Our Country (the masses of America) has to be active and vigilant against these small yet very vocal and destructive groups.

"At the stage between apathy and dependency, men always turn in fear to economic and political panaceas. New conditions, it is claimed, require new remedies. Under such circumstances, the competent citizen is certainly not a fool if he insists upon using the compass of history when forced to sail uncharted seas. Usually so-called new remedies are not new at all. *Compulsory* planned economy, for example, was tried by the Chinese some three milleniums ago, and by the Romans in the early centuries of the Christian era. It was applied in Germany, Italy and Russia long before the present war broke out. Yet it is being seriously advocated today as a solution of our economic problems in the United States. Its proponents confidently assert that government can successfully plan and control all major business activity in the nation, and still not interfere with our political freedom and our hard-won civil and religious liberties. The lessons of history all point in exactly the reverse direction."

Henning W. Prentis, Industrial Management in a Republic,

Term Limits

Implementing term limits for elected officials will have a major positive impact on representatives. They will be able to tackle hard issues today, without fear of re-election. The major benefit from term limits is that it will keep lobbyists jockeying for position with a moving target of representatives. Lobbyists and special interest groups have attached themselves to career politicians and have figured out ways around the laws to influence our lawmakers. Career politicians are extremely susceptible to being persuaded/bought-off by special interest groups.

Why are term limits not being implemented when all of America would benefit? Let's look at some incentives lobbyists and special interest groups provide career politicians:

- Pay legislators directly or indirectly to get legislators to vote a particular way
- Promise positions to legislators when they retire or are "fired" (not reelected) by the American public
- Raise money for the representatives' campaigns to keep them in place to serve the lobbyists and vote in favor of their positions

Why else would a person spend *millions* of dollars to get a $180,000 per year job? There is no logic to this math unless you are a career candidate in the Senate or Congress. It is for this reason term limits are such a critical issue and should be foremost on the public's agenda.

"Over the last twenty years, term limits have been one of the most widely debated issues across the nation. Americans have become sick of their local politicians who are seeking nothing more than to hold a seat for twenty years, until they have a shot at running for Congress.

In fifteen states across America, citizens have voted overwhelmingly to place term limits on their state legislatures. Two of these states have used activist judges to remove term limits.

Thirty-seven states place some form of term limits on their governor and other constitutional offices.

Polling shows that term limits is just as popular in the states in which they exist as they were when the laws were first passed.

These alarming numbers cause fear for career politicians, which is why they are the ones who seek to eliminate term limits. US Term Limits continues to be the leader in blocking politicians, lobbyists and special interests from repealing term limits for their own personal gain.

Nine of the ten largest cities in America have term limits on their city council and/or mayor."

From www.termlimits.org

Government Salaries

Why in the world with mounting debt and being in the middle of a "Great Recession" would the federal government be growing and prospering? Analyze the comments and figures below:

"The number of federal workers earning six-figure salaries has exploded during the recession, according to a USA TODAY analysis of federal salary data.

Federal employees making salaries of $100,000 or more jumped from 14% to 19% of civil servants during the *recession's first 18 months* — and that's before overtime pay and bonuses are counted.

Federal workers are enjoying an extraordinary boom time — in pay and hiring — during a recession that has cost 7.3 million jobs in the private sector.

The highest-paid federal employees are doing best of all on salary increases. Defense Department civilian employees earning

$150,000 or more increased from 1,868 in December 2007 to **10,100 in June 2009,** the most recent figure available.

When the recession started, the Transportation Department had only one person earning a salary of $170,000 or more. Eighteen months later, 1,690 employees had salaries above $170,000."

By Dennis Cauchon, USA TODAY

The following chart shows the discrepancy of jobs and salaries from the government to the private sector. These figures are mind blowing considering we are in a recession and the unbalanced budget our government operates under...

Federal Workers Earning Increases 12/07 - 6/09;

$100K +	$150K +	$170K +
382,758 (+46%)	66,538 (+119%)	22,157 (+93%)

Note: The number of highly paid federal employees has soared since the recession began in December 2007

Jobs Gained/Lost 12/07 - 6/09;

Federal Gov't	State & Local Gov't	Private Sector
192,700 (+9.8%)	33,000 (+2%)	-7.3 million (-6.2%)

Pay Raises 12/07 - 6/09;

Federal Gov't	State & Local Gov't	Private Sector
$71,206 (+6.6%)	$54,101 (3.9%)	$40,331 (+3.9%)

Notes:
+ The average government worker makes $30,000 more than the average private sector employee!!
+ The federal government is adding jobs this year at a rate of nearly 10,000 a month - The fastest pace since the 1960s when Medicare and Medicaid were created
+ The average Federal salary has grown nearly twice as fast as private pay during the recession

Office of Personnel Management; USA TODAY analysis

Burden on the Taxpayers

Let's analyze the burden of this huge government workforce on the average working citizen.

Private Sector Stats:

The US Population is now around 304,000,000 people. As of April 2009, there are **154,731,000** in the *civilian* workforce.

Government Supported Employees:

Local, State, Federal approx	20,000,000
Military (Active & reserves) approx	2,303,000
Welfare Recipients approx	4,000,000
Postal Jobs approx	800,000
Total Approximate:	**27,000,000**

This does not include all the consultants employed by the Government (DOE has over 100,000 by itself!). It does not include the unemployed (around 15,000,000) the government is subsidizing nor the social security benefits it is dispersing. Hence, we are showing you a very conservative number in this analysis.

Results:

27,000,000 government employees / 154,731,000 civilian employees = **17.5%**.

The real number probably is around 42,500,000 individuals the government is supporting during this recession (with unemployment and a stab at consultants).

42,500,000 government wage earners / 154,731,000 civilian employees = **27%**

That is not a sustainable model of operation and has to be corrected. No wonder our national debt is out of control.

Restructuring Ideas

When the forefathers of America were configuring the government in the late 1700's, telephones, email, airplanes, computers, etc. did not exist. The newly formed country was primarily based on agriculture and had a much slower lifestyle than today. Two hundred plus years later, our society has unbelievable technology streamlining our businesses to make them much more efficient. The US Government has done the opposite by creating a haven where it is hard to get fired and easy to collect a paycheck. The government is wrought with inefficiencies. The government needs to act like a business and operate with a balanced budget, rid its debt, restructure, and have performance monitoring systems just as a private business must do to remain successful.

The government is trained not to save, but to use their allocated budgets completely. If a government department has leftover money at the end of the year, it will use it up or it will not get the same budget allocation the next budget year - "Use it or lose it." Many states had surpluses before the "2009 Great Recession" but failed to save surpluses because of this "use it or lose it" system. Now in the "Great Recession" some states are battling bankruptcy. This type of operational practice has to be stopped. Politicians get popular during the "Fat" years, but cost their constituents dearly during the lean years. Fiscal responsibility needs to be monitored and enforced.

With the use of modern technology, we could streamline and then automate processes to create "National Best Practices" for:

+ Towns/Cities
+ Counties
+ States

Service providers, after working in a specialized industry over time, begin to master their industry client's desired functionalities, processes, and business. A friend of mine owns a web site development company which has served many Chamber of Commerce businesses for a long time. The time his company has invested in this deep vertical market has resulted in a thorough knowledge of their business. His company understands the business of the Chamber of Commerce better than most of the Chamber of Commerce directors. A Chamber of Commerce can purchase his web template and adapt it to look unique and actually gain functionality and provide more benefits to its members. This can be done at a fraction of the cost of developing one from scratch. This same model should be used across government entities to save taxpayers' money.

"Best practices" processing should be achieved and automated at each level of government. Then we can then look vertically to the next level and see what processes make sense to consolidate. Back-end office processes (accounting, data management, information services, etc.) might work better when consolidated between towns and counties or counties and states. Automating processes and back office work does not impact the representation at any level of government. We are not advocating abolishing local government or local representation but abolishing inefficient systems/processes.

As government functions become streamlined and automated, it will be easier to report to the public and handle issues. The gray areas of self-serving/interest groups disappear as transparency increases. Fewer levels of supporting infrastructure, and people interacting within the infrastructure, means less empires are established (overhead) and less confusion.

The government should establish a "Scrubbing" team that could be comprised of non-partisan consultants and auditing professionals. This group should have the highest security clearance and be able to work inside any department in the federal government and move freely between departments. The group should report to Congress behind closed doors to report the findings for cost savings by utilizing streamlining, automating and/or consolidating opportunities.

The government employs many consulting companies already, but they are engaged in specific departments for specific tasks. The obvious goal of consultants is billable hours and security, so they burrow into their host to thrive as long as possible in a parasitic relationship. To make sure this "Scrubbing" team is contained, there should be a cap on the consultants engaged and a specific charter for its directives and deliverables with timeframes.

When a business is in financial trouble, it uses cost-cutting measures for survival. The government, established to serve its citizens, should act in the same manner.

Representative Overhead

We have representatives at all levels of the government: towns/cities, counties, states, and federal. The Federal Government has five hundred thirty five members of the House and Senate. If you add up all the representatives at the state level it is over *six thousand!* The question then becomes - Do we really need that many representatives when we can disseminate information so well via internet news, radio, TV, etc? What are the costs of supporting so many representatives and are they all needed to make our country operable? Maybe we should send one or two representatives home from the House of Representatives on all levels... do we really need that many law makers? Perhaps we should redistrict and streamline voting districts to cut some of the fat out of government layers.

Just a note concerning our representatives' compensation: Congress should no longer be able to vote for their *own pay raises.* **Since when does an employee tell the employer how much he is going to make?**

It should be voted on by the people. Congress also should not receive a lifetime pension plan, but instead an opportunity to work after they have finished serving the American public. This change will cause our representatives to think twice about raising taxes. They too will be responsible for paying these taxes when their term limits are completed and they rejoin the work force.

In Switzerland, they have a direct democracy where the public meets to vote on issues. Voting can be done by counting hands in the public square or sent in by mail or email. This would have been difficult in the past for the US, but using the internet the United States could move in that direction.

Government representatives have a tendency to walk away from the central stance of Americans once elected. It would be quite a transition, but can you imagine the "Reality" show where the citizens are informed every Monday evening of the topics up for vote and could actually vote over the internet? It would be very hard for the special interest groups and lobbyists to sway that many people...

Who Should Vote

"Two centuries ago, a somewhat obscure Scotsman named Tytler made this profound observation: "A democracy cannot exist as a permanent form of government. It can only exist until the majority discovers it can vote itself largess (gifts) out of the public treasury. After that, the majority always votes for the candidate promising the most benefits with the result the democracy collapses because of the loose fiscal policy ensuing, always to be followed by a dictatorship, then a monarchy."
Elmer T. Peterson, www.lorencollins.net/tytler.html

"Paradoxically enough, the release of initiative and enterprise made possible by popular self-government ultimately generates

disintegrating forces from within. Again and again after freedom has brought opportunity and some degree of plenty, the competent become selfish, luxury-loving and complacent, the incompetent and the unfortunate grow envious and covetous, and all three groups turn aside from the hard road of freedom to worship the Golden Calf of economic security. **The historical cycle seems to be: From bondage to spiritual faith; from spiritual faith to courage; from courage to liberty; from liberty to abundance; from abundance to selfishness; from selfishness to apathy; from apathy to dependency; and from dependency back to bondage once more."**
Prentis' Speech "Industrial Management in a Republic," 3/18/1943

When creating the United States Government, the argument of who should have the right to vote was heated. James Madison defined the problem:

"The right of suffrage (right to vote) is a fundamental Article in Republican Constitutions. The regulation of it is, at the same time, a task of peculiar delicacy. Allow the right exclusively to property, and the rights of persons may be oppressed... . Extend it equally to all, and the rights of property ...may be overruled by a majority without property...."

James Madison

People who have something to lose, hence something to fight for, should be more involved in decision-making for the country. If one has nothing to lose, there tends to be apathy and he will bend toward perks out of the "Public Treasury." Voting is a privilege fought for by our forefathers and preserved every time the country engages in war. It is not something to be taken lightly, so limiting voting to people who actually have a stake in the country should not be shocking.

Instead of looking at property to justify a person's right to vote, the country should look at taxes. If an individual is paying taxes (being productive in society and contributing to the country), they should have the right to vote. Citizens who do not pay taxes, should not have the opportunity to tip the "Public Treasury" to their benefit. In order to register to vote, *citizens* would have to go through a registration process every tax season. This would help prevent future "ACORN" like attempts at rigging elections using the apathetic and dependent sectors of our society to swing votes. Representatives buying votes achieves only more control (bondage) by our Government.

> "People who receive public tax money for their livelihood are dependent upon the entity from which they receive their stipend. Therefore, if these same people are eligible to vote, they will elect those who will most likely continue to support them financially. This is the insidious plan that has been in place since the 1960's. Enslave people financially and they will vote against the interest of the masses for their own benefit. A suckling pig will not voluntarily diminish its food source.
>
> The term disfranchisement was used even in 1787. The term was not invented in 2000 when some falsely accused George W. Bush of "stealing an election". The term was then used in regards to placing qualifications on the right to vote. The term of "taxation without representation" was a long used battle cry in the young nation and part of the reason for the revolution. Just as bad, however, is "representation without taxation".
>
> Troy LaPlante, HubPages

Summary

The way our government is operating and growing with mounting debt to stay functional is not a sustainable system. Like business, the government needs to restructure, streamline, automate, work with balanced budgets and rid debt. This needs to be a part of the solution equation for the country. Can you imagine how prosperous our nation would be if we operated with only a balanced budget and it was debt free?

CHAPTER 6

The Crisis

The World will not evolve past its current state of crisis by using the same thinking that created the situation.

Albert Einstein

Before sharing our solution to empower America's energy independence and a strong economy, we are going to present some background on the road we traveled to find answers. We were amazed at the logjams and government workers avoiding the hard questions. There is a veil over our government that is misdirecting our nation's prosperity. The following trail outlines communications and research over a three-year period and give you a glimpse of what is going on behind the scenes in our government. We need to look objectively at what has caused the stifling of ingenuity and creativity in the private sector of energy.

In this Chapter we will look at:
- Paths To Discoveries
    - Local Representation
    - Senate Subcommittee on Energy

- o Department of Energy
- o The Bipartisan Policy Center
- ✦ Climate Change
- ✦ Process of Status Quo

Paths Of Discoveries

Three years ago when gas prices were hovering around four dollars per gallon and as the economy began to stutter people began to question why we were in such a predicament. How could the United States government, with so many committees, departments, and agencies on energy, be so ineffective with reasonable solutions. The government should have been working on solutions since the very first energy crisis in the 70's. However, here we are 33 years later in the same situation. The obvious solution back then, as it is today, is to cut energy dependency quickly, create jobs, and lower the cost of fuel leading to an economic recovery.

In the quest for logical answers, the first place to ask these questions would be with local representatives...

Local Representation:

US Senator Richard Burr (NC) and US Senator Kay Hagan (NC), who should have a very orderly explanation of the country's efforts to recover from this energy debacle, were called over 30 times in hopes of reasonable explanations. A reasonable approach for a solution was not available and the Representatives did not even define the problem clearly. This was very frustrating especially since Senator Burr served on the *US Senate Committee on Energy and Natural Resources.*

We contacted another Congressperson's office in North Carolina as well. The aids told us they were referencing FactCheck and Snopes! These are not scientific organizations, but organizations correcting politicians and urban legends. In 2005, this representative joined the *Energy and Commerce Committee*, so we thought this office would be on board with a real energy solution. Please understand we respect our representation in government, but they might not be operating outside the veil of misinformation.

Senate Subcommittee on Energy:

Moving on from the local Representatives, we inquired at the Senate Committee on Energy for answers. At the time of contact, there were thirteen Democrats and ten Republicans on the committee. Each received direct phone calls to get their position on using America's fossil fuel resources. The Democrats definitely did not want to drill and the Republicans did not believe we could drill with government restrictions that were currently in place. The Democrats reported that even if we did drill, it would be five to ten years before we saw any fruit from that labor. Even if that were true, which it is not, would that be a good reason to delay? As soon as drilling starts and a plan is on the table, the money starts to flow and the economy begins to improve. Please feel free to call them at 202-224-4971 and see if they are getting closer to a logical solution.

Department of Energy (DOE):

The next logical stop was The Department of Energy for real solutions. The Department of Energy was established in 1977 to ensure our nuclear weapons and facilities are safe and that we would become and remain energy independent as a nation. This organization was established by the Carter administration during the Iran Oil Crisis to reduce foreign energy dependence so our country would never be crippled again. Look how far we have come.

Following is the mission statement right off of the Department of Energy's web site:

"The Department of Energy's overarching mission is to advance the national, economic, and energy security of the United States; to promote scientific and technological innovation in support of that mission; and to ensure the environmental cleanup of the national nuclear weapons complex. The Department's strategic goals to achieve the mission are designed to deliver results along five strategic themes:

1. Energy Security: Promoting America's energy security through reliable, clean, and affordable energy
2. Nuclear Security: Ensuring America's nuclear security
3. Scientific Discovery and Innovation: Strengthening U.S. scientific discovery, economic competitiveness, and improving quality of life through innovations in science and technology
4. Environmental Responsibility: Protecting the environment by providing a responsible resolution to the environmental legacy of nuclear weapons production
5. Management Excellence: Enabling the mission through sound management"

www.energy.gov/about

The DOE even has an active environmentalist, Secretary Chu, as its leader now. Please look at his resume on the DOE web site:

"Dr. Chu has devoted his recent scientific career to the search for new solutions to our energy challenges and stopping global *climate change* – a mission he continues with even *greater* urgency as Secretary of Energy. He is charged with helping implement President Obama's ambitious agenda to *invest in alternative and renewable energy*, end our addiction to foreign oil, address the *global climate crisis* and create millions of new jobs. ... motivated by his deep interest in *climate change*, he has recently led the Lawrence Berkeley National Lab in pursuit of new alternative and renewable energies."

www.energy.gov/organization/dr_steven_chu.htm

Because of the leaders in our government, any logical relief from our national fossil fuel reserves is not an option. So we continue to import and be dependent on fossil fuels from foreign countries and pretend America does not have any solutions until renewable energy is eventually affordable. We have been in this situation for over 33 years and we are not changing anytime soon. If it were up to our DOE, we would be obeying the Copenhagen agenda and paying big money to the world economies for our giant carbon footprint. Not a smart move for our energy independence and economic security.

The Department of Energy, paid for by American tax dollars, should be working very hard on short-term and long-term solutions to ensure America is reaching its potential to be energy independent. This could not be farther from the truth. The Department of Energy currently employs sixteen thousand federal employees as well as over one hundred thousand outside contractors. Currently we import **sixty-one percent** of our oil from foreign countries, and this figure remains pretty stable. So over the course of thirty-three years of operation, we are actually worse off than during the first energy crisis when we established the Department of Energy for change.

We are still dependent on foreign countries because the Department of Energy is really not about energy anymore but has become the second Environmental Protection Agency. Our opinion is that the DOE should be changed into a Nuclear Protection Agency only. This would scale down the employees and contractors to support the critical needs of nuclear management. It would also release our natural resources so that free enterprise can work on energy solutions – the government is sure not helping. This would help cut national budget expenses.

Unfortunately, we did not get any answers from the Department of Energy. But a person at the DOE did mention another committee in the hunt for solutions: the Bipartisan Policy Center.

i. **The Bipartisan Policy Center:**

Bipartisan Policy Center defined from its web site:

> "The Bipartisan Policy Center (BPC) is a non-profit organization that was established in 2007 by former Senate Majority Leaders Howard Baker, Tom Daschle, Bob Dole and George Mitchell to develop and promote solutions that can attract public support and political momentum in order to achieve real progress."
>
> **www.bipartisanpolicy.org/about**

The Center was started by Jason Grumet. He lured George Mitchell, Tom Daschle, Bob Dole, and Howard Baker on as advisory board members to add credence to the Center's point of view when reporting to Congress (testifying). Let's zero in on the National Commission on Energy Policy which is now under the Bipartisan Policy Center's umbrella. With a title like that, you would think this group would be a star headliner madly researching our best avenues to create energy independence. Here is their charge:

> "Since 2002, the National Commission on Energy Policy--a bipartisan group of 20 of the nation's leading energy experts representing the highest ranks of industry, government, academia, labor, consumer and environmental protection—has been advising Congress, the Executive Branch, States and other policymakers regarding long-term U.S. policy."
>
> **www.bipartisanpolicy.org**

The problem with the testimony of these groups is that they are influenced by the two large foundations that pay the salaries of the employees in the center. These two foundations are **The William and Flora Hewlett Foundation** and the **Rockefeller Foundation.** Gratefully, an assistant from the Bipartisan Policy Center's office sent their 2007 tax returns showing that the Center received over *eleven million dollars* from

70

these two foundations! Both of these groups are global warming and environmentally driven. Would you bite the hand that feeds you?

The Foundations' Mission Statements:

> The William and Flora Hewlett Foundation has been making grants since 1967 to solve social and **environmental problems** at home and around the world.
>
> www.hewlett.org/about

> The Rockefeller Foundation supports work that expands opportunity and strengthens resilience to social, economic, health and **environmental challenges**—affirming its pioneering philanthropic mission since 1913 to "promote the well-being" of humanity.
>
> www.rockefellerfoundation.org/about-us

If you want to continue to get paid by these foundations, you should state their positions often and without regard to America's energy needs and that is exactly what the Bipartisan Policy Center does. They toe the line for the foundations. This Bipartisan Policy Center has nothing to do with energy or job creation for the American public.

If you look at the "Commissioners" on the Bipartisan Policy Center's National Commission on Energy Policy (NCEP), you will notice that most of them have a common background: **environmentalist.** You would think energy experts would be better equipped to lead this charge instead of environmentalists - just a wild thought. The NCEP testifies before congress, and has since 2002, on questions concerning energy. They also worked with Congress in 2007 on the key aspects of the Energy Independence and Security Act of 2007. The title for that act is misleading since it has nothing to do with energy and everything to do with global warming and the environment. Following is an excerpt from their work on the 2007 Energy Policy Recommendations:

"In brief, this short list of priority items calls for addressing the demand as well as the supply side of the oil security equation; advancing a timely and meaningful response to the problem of *global climate change*; expanding on current efforts to promote both increased energy efficiency and a greater diversity of domestic energy supply options; and substantially increasing federal investment in energy technology research, development, demonstration, and early deployment. Going forward, the Commission intends further work in all of these areas as part of an ongoing effort to refine its understanding of key issues and to continue informing the public policy debate."

Energy Policy Recommendations to the President and the 110th Congress Apr. 19, 2007

Is this committee really after non-biased logical energy solutions to better the Country or supporting environmental initiatives?

Following are the Co-Chairs for the NCEP and parts of their biographies:

William K. Reilly: Administrator of the *U.S. Environmental Protection Agency* (1989-1993), and president of the World Wildlife Fund (1985-1989). He served as head of the US delegation to the Earth Summit at Rio in 1992

Susan Tierney: Dr. Tierney is Chairman of the Board of the Energy Foundation; is a director on the boards of the Catalytica Energy Systems Inc., EPRI Inc., the Energy Innovations Institute, *Clean Air-Cool Planet*, and the North East States Clean Air Foundation. Prior to her work at the DOE, Dr. Tierney served as *Secretary of Environmental Affairs* for the Commonwealth of Massachusetts, overseeing five agencies, and was responsible for the Boston Harbor Clean Up, Clean Air Act implementation, *emissions trading regulations, environmental impact reviews*, and energy facility sitting.

Based on the nation's current energy track record and results over the last eight years, this group should not be testifying and advising America's energy policy to our government. It should be advising on environmental issues instead of energy issues. Give the Bipartisan Policy Center and the National Commission on Energy Policy a call to talk to them yourself: 202-204-2400. Ask them about their motivations and the over eleven million dollars they receive from their sponsors. Call Paul Brest, President of the Hewlett Foundation, to get his opinions on Global Warming and America's economy.

Climate Change

We already went into great detail on the background of Climate Change and CO2 Cap and Trade earlier in the book. In summary, there is a lot of money betting on climate change and CO2 Cap and Trade. The proponents of these movements have already made a fortune and have created a religious atmosphere where it is forbidden to blaspheme against the movement. However, the facts are pointing in the opposite direction but the deacons of these environmental movements are holding on as long as they can for financial gain. If they can get the Cap and Trade passed, they stand to benefit in the *billions* of dollars. It is extremely essential that our government does not pass laws to hinder our energy independence in the short term or tax our economy even more. This is a fight we cannot afford to lose. Fossil fuels are not the enemy of the environment.

Process of Status Quo:

Following is a synopsis of what has been happening over the last 33 years to move us toward energy independence:

1. Interior Secretary (now Salazar) approves opening up federal land to begin exploration
2. Congress approves or disapproves after consulting with internal committees and special interest groups.
3. Motion comes back to the Congressional floor with **earmarks** added
4. Committees (including the Bipartisan Policy Center) testifies before Congress on the environmental impacts of fossil fuels and renewable energy.
5. Congress decides not to move forward with bills where drilling is involved
6. Media reports on the future environmental damages of drilling for energy
7. Gas prices go from $4.10/gallon to $2.75/gallon
8. American public feels good about new gas prices
9. Congress ignores drilling initiatives and all is well until the next energy crisis

The reason we never achieve real answers for energy independence is that there is no sense of urgency until we reach another energy crisis where fuel prices go through the roof. It is a cycle that we have gone through for 35 years and will continue until the government will let America tap its own resources. The nay-sayers who do not want to drill for natural gas and oil say it will take 10 years to get the product out of the earth. This is America - just get out of the way and let free enterprise motivate companies and workers and watch how fast this will go. America mobilized and established a war machine almost immediately out of nothing when engaged in WWII. America can do it again - this is a war for our future.

Regulation is crippling America's ability to be financially successful. Congress tells energy companies when they can drill, where they can drill, and how they can drill. Eighty percent of the lands where we have vast energy resources are **federally controlled.** The resources from these lands would eliminate foreign oil dependency and end our financial hostage status. This means government action is required to remove the barriers to prosperity.

Summary

It is difficult to break the veil of misinformation our government is operating under. The needs of the American public are not being addressed by our politicians. We do not need another committee in Washington, DC, to be successful in finding energy and economic solutions. We need people in government who know how to run businesses and leaders who can put a logical action plan together that the American public can get excited about.

CHAPTER 7

The Solution

*No people will tamely surrender their Liberties, nor can any
be easily subdued, when knowledge is diffused and Virtue
is preserved. On the contrary, when people are universally
ignorant, and debauched in their manners, they will sink under
their own weight without the aid of foreign invaders.*

Samuel Adams

In 2005, Burma encountered Cyclone Nargis which created massive damage and flooding from a huge tsunami. Over 75,000 people died and many thousands were left homeless. The world, led by the United States, immediately offered relief in the way of food and supplies, but the military Juntas blocked the supplies from reaching the people because of their suspicions of the West. This caused many to starve and go without drinking water even though all the supplies were right at their fingertips. Instead, thousands died needlessly because of starvation and contaminated drinking water from puddles where dead bodies lay. The problem was not the supply chain, but those who kept the supplies from being used! The same problem that plagued Burma exists in the United States right now except the supplies are oil and natural gas instead of food and water.

The only difference in the two situations is that instead of a military Junta stopping supplies, it is a misinformed government and a strong group of special interest parties who are keeping America in bondage concerning our own energy resources and a prospering economy.

We would like to tell you that the solution to our financial and energy problems is easy to fix, but it will take a strong will from the people of the United States and a new direction from our government for us to achieve financial prosperity once again. If we could remove the climate change initiative and all the politics surrounding that movement, we could give you wonderful news of how exciting America's financial and energy future could be and how to get there.

<u>Where The Resources Are</u>

America has been at a standstill concerning new major oil discoveries for more than thirty years. The source of today's domestic oil production comes from over one hundred fifty thousand wells from all parts of the country. The average well produces fifteen barrels a day.

Let's look at the facts, with no opinion thrown in, to see what our nation's real capabilities are for energy independence according to the US Energy Information Administration (EIA), US Geological Survey Group (USGS), and the North Dakota Geological Survey group. These groups have no agendas but report facts. If we use the conservative estimates of the USGS and the EIA, the following are the oil reserves in three major federal land locations:

The Bakken Formation   510 billion barrels
(North & South Dakota, and Montana)

Green River shale oil basins   750 billion barrels
(Colorado, Wyoming, and Utah)

ANWR or 1002 region of Alaska	17 billion barrels
Potential Domestic Oil:	**1,277 billion barrels**

The United States uses roughly 7.14 billion barrels of oil a year so let's do the math:

1,277 billion barrels in oil reserves / 7.14 billion barrels per year =

179 years of domestic oil reserves

We have not even mentioned the abundance of natural gas deposits in these regions – huge amounts. We are concerned right now with importing energy and boosting our economy away from foreign suppliers.

We have more oil than the **entire Middle East** put together, but we continue to ignore our resources because of this veil of misinformation over our government. Remember the forces we exposed earlier who are working against our nations' natural resources and economic prosperity.

After thirty-three years of trying to be energy independent through the Department of Energy, the US could be independent from foreign oil in a couple years. Plus we have enough reserves to become a large exporter. This is such good news that our citizens should be stampeding congress to open these lands up.

Jobs Impact

Currently the oil and gas industries support 9.2 million jobs in the United States. We have been drilling in the same locations for over one hundred years and have not opened up new lands to create new initiatives. If we opened up the 40% of lands that have not been drilled, we could create another nine million high paying jobs reducing unemployment rolls at the welfare centers across America.

America has not created a new oil refinery in over thirty years. The investment for a new refinery is over two billion dollars. It is a daunting commitment of capital in this environment when the oil industry is continuously under attack from special interest groups. America needs refineries to support its current oil consumption and these refineries will infuse capital and generate work to boost our economy.

Implementation

Here is a step-by-step action plan which, if implemented, could be the solution to harvesting our domestic resources:

1. Interior Secretary (Salazar) releases federal land for exploration
2. Congress concurs
3. Federal land is put out to bid to oil companies
4. Three contracts will be established with **domestic** oil companies
5. American ingenuity builds new refineries for oil and natural gas

Results:

- Nine million jobs are created by keeping energy jobs in America
- Gas prices drop dramatically at the pump due to increased supply
- The US wealth transfer is halted to foreign countries
- America is able to export oil to foreign countries decreasing our debt structure
- State revenues go up due to oil and natural gas production

These initiatives will get the ball rolling, but now we need to talk about how to get cash flowing into this new dynamic. Let's think about a common sense approach with a logical sequence.

If the government establishes public/private partnerships with at least three large oil companies on the federal lands, that would infuse immediate cash into our government. The trick is not to let the government spend it. For example, Exxon is worth over five hundred billion dollars and just bought out XTO Energy for a reported forty one billion dollars. Our government needs to lease this land and place stipulations on timeframes for drilling. This will force oil companies into action and the government can gain revenue from the lease and from the quantity of oil extracted from the land. The formula would have to work for both the oil companies and our country since the oil companies have to be willing to invest in new infrastructure. The additional revenue stream for our country could be tremendous.

If the government is willing to lease 40% of its land, how much do you think that would bring into the government overnight? Maybe three hundred billion dollars?!? The average cost to extract a barrel of oil in the US is $8.35 per barrel (EIA- Crude Oil Production Last Updated: March 2009). If a barrel of oil sells for seventy plus dollars on the international market, there is a little room to bring the costs down for our economy and reap some profit for both the oil companies and the US Government. If the US uses seven plus billion barrels of oil per year (EIA), and out of that we get sixty percent from federal lands (displacing foreign oil imports), that equals over four and a half billion barrels of oil the US could make revenue on. Let's say, for example, we place a ten dollar "profit sharing" amount on every barrel, the government would be able to take in an extra forty five billion dollars of revenue per year just from our country's usage - not counting oil that is exported.

Benefits from Solution

Now that the US Government has some money up front and a new revenue stream, let's look at how the government needs to act to benefit our country and not squander the money. We should invest it in our future, such as:

1. One billion dollars goes into a fund called the "Nobel Energy Prize" to be paid to the first company or individual who comes up with a legitimate cost-effective alternative energy method that works as voted on by a non-biased energy group. This winner will be given a fast track by the powers in government to implement this plan into a working method to be used by the American public. This new technology/system cannot be sidelined by a purchasing company who normally sidelines its competition.

2. Use a portion of the money to increase fireman, policeman, and teacher pay to reflect the value of these honorable professions. This will help in recruiting good candidates to fill these roles in the future.

3. Allocate money to fund families who make $50 thousand or less per year for wellness care. This will not fund drugs, only physicals and yearly visits.

4. The remainder of money raised should be split between the national debt and a new federal emergency fund. This fund cannot be touched unless our **term limit congress** votes in a 75% affirmative vote to use these funds in an emergency situation.

5. Depending on the severity of the economy when this solution is implemented, the government could stop withholding taxes for a period of time so Americans can get a little relief, feel good about this new momentum, and start spending again.

Here are a few recommendations for our government. These will help tear down the wall between our government and the people of this country by moving forward in a fiscally responsible manner:

1. Congress institutes term limits. We already talked about this in detail, but this is essential if we are going to have fair representation in our government.
2. Need to cut out government overhead and manage it as a business. The constituents are the clients not the slaves.
3. Congress has to balance their budgets at the state and federal levels. America cannot afford to operate on a Ponzi-scheme.
4. There needs to be a plan for national debt elimination. Every prosperous year in the American economy should reduce debts and also save resources for the lean years. Our economy is cyclical, so we should prepare for the lean years instead of the "use it or lose it" type of budget management system in place right now.
5. Need to restructure the government infrastructure at every level. "Best practices" should be implemented for all towns, cities, counties, states, and federal governments. A "cleansing" consulting team should be implemented to be a watchdog for inefficient government processes.
6. If you would like to live in this country and enjoy benefits, you must do it legally. We are all immigrants to this country, but the American taxpayer can no longer shoulder the load of illegal workers/families who do not pay into the system but are allowed to use it. Many illegal workers would need to register and pay taxes. America needs to implement a system to handle these folks.
7. Restructure the voting privilege. If you do not pay taxes, you do not vote. After every tax season voters will be registered for the next round of elections.

Each of the above initiatives could bring our country back to greatness and prosperity. Teachers, firemen, and policemen would be working for good wages. Our classrooms would be excelling with well-paid merit teachers. Our politicians would become honorable again with a servant's heart for the people. And finally, the tax burden on the back of the American family could be reduced greatly by using our plentiful resources sitting beneath our feet. We must also reduce the size and inefficiency of government at every level.

Summary

It sounds like we are taking a step backwards from the "renewable energy" charge that has become so popular, but in reality there are only two options our country has right now:

1. Continue to pay for foreign oil while we continue to supplement renewable energy (both are cost drains) and hoping renewable energy will become affordable and competitive with fossil fuels. We have been waiting over 35 years already...
2. Drill and use our natural resources as an interim solution until a better more economical energy system is discovered/created. This solution is not a cost drain but infuses money into our economy until we can find a better solution.

It does not matter what political, social, environmental, or financial views you have, as soon as you get in a car or take a plane you are participating in and supporting the oil based economy. It seems logical to tap into the oil industry because it does not need to be subsidized by our government to gain energy independence and to stabilize our economy. Every oil rich country around the globe has already opted for this solution...

CHAPTER 8

Where we go from here

I believe there are more instances of the abridgment of the freedom of the people by gradual and silent encroachments of those in power than by violent and sudden usurpations.

James Madison, speech, Virginia Convention, 1788

He who desires, but acts not, breeds pestilence.

William Blake

When Rome started its decline as the world power, its citizens were distracted from the important issues affecting their society. One large distraction was the entertainment in their coliseums. As the country decayed in morals/values, public health, political corruption, unemployment, inflation, technology, and military demise, the population was watching and cheering on their heroes in the stadiums. Is America following the same pattern? Are the masses of Americans more concerned about the Super Bowl and American Idol than its political and economic future? As concerned citizens, we need to focus on our

Country's direction and take *action*. We believe we are at a crossroads where we have to correct the momentum our government has gained in power and size.

Grass Roots Movement:

We need a grass roots movement for change in America. Our government does not represent the masses anymore, but has turned into a giant that we feel is out of our control. This is quite evident considering they just passed the Health Care Bill which America does not want. Washington is not listening to its constituents and this needs to change. We need to bond together and create a loud voice that the government cannot ignore. The truth needs to be clear and the options laid out for the American people to choose. There are enough topics for just about everyone to find a passion to speak out on. Some of the topics for action in summary from this book are:

- Negating Climate Change and Cap and Trade legislation
- Addressing the US National Debt
- Government Overhaul Initiatives
  - o Term Limits
  - o Government Salaries
  - o Restructuring Ideas
  - o Representative Overhead
  - o Voting Privileges
  - o Government Balanced Budgets
- Harvesting Domestic Energy Supplies

Action Steps:

> *The only thing necessary for the triumph [of evil] is for good men to do nothing.*

> *Edmund Burke*

Contact Your Representative:

Well, as you can tell through our experience, contacting your representative has minimal impact. PLEASE call them, but you will probably be talking to an aid and they will screen the message if it is not in the representative's best interest. Calling and telling your representative they need to take a pay cut and stop their benefits is probably not going to go over very well – we tried. We need to have our voices heard and this is the first point of contact you should take action on. Please do not stop with just a phone call, but continue to call and also take additional action steps.

Contact Representatives in the Oil Rich States:

Every congressperson who lives in an oil, natural gas, or energy rich state should be extremely vocal for the regulatory noose to be released from the neck of his or her state. Some of the key states containing great resources in oil and natural gas are served by the following Senators. Give them a call and tell them to begin securing America's energy independence:

John Barrasso®- Wyoming- 202-224-6441
Max Baucus (D)- Montana- 202-224-2651
Mark Begich (D)- Alaska- 202-224-3004
Michael Bennet(D)- Colorado- 202-224-5444
Barbara Boxer (D)- California-202-224-3553
Richard Burr ®- North Carolina-202-224-3154
Tom Coburn ®- Oklahoma- 202-224-5754
Susan Collins ®- Maine- 202-224-2523
Kent Conrad (D)- North Dakota- 202-224-2043
> Please note, Senator Conrad's state is in the black financially because of successful limited drilling of oil in the Bakken formation and the revenues his state has been able to raise because of the efforts.
John Cornyn ®- Texas- 202-224-2934
Byron Dorgan (D)- North Dakota- 202-224-2551
Michael Enzi ®- Wyoming- 202-224-3424

Diane Feinstein (D)- California- 202-224-5641
Kay Hagan (D)- North Carolina- 202-224-6342
Orrin Hatch ® - Utah- 202-224-5251
Kay Bailey Hutchison ® -Texas- 202-224-5922
James Inhofe ®- Oklahoma- 202-224-4721
Tim Johnson (D)- South Dakota- 202-224-5842
Mary Landrieu (D)- Louisiana- 202-224-5824
George LeMieux ®- Florida- 202-224-3041
Lisa Murkowski ®- Alaska- 202-224-6665
Patty Murray (D) – Washington- 202-224-2621
Bill Nelson (D) – Florida- 202-224-5274
Jeff Merkley (D) – Oregon- 202-224-3753
Harry Reid (D)- Nevada- 202-224-3542
John Rockefeller (D) – West Virginia- 202-224-6472
Olympia Snowe ® - Maine- 202-224-5344
Jon Tester (D) – Montana- 202-224-2644
John Thune ® - South Dakota- 202-224-2321
Mark Udall (D) – Colorado- 202-224-5941
Tom Udall (D) – New Mexico- 202-224-6621
David Vitter ® - Louisiana- 202-224-4623
Ron Wyden (D) – Oregon – 202-224-5244

www.TrueResults4US.Org:

This is a new web site formed to give Americans a chance to:

- ✦ Voice opinions
- ✦ Share information
- ✦ Identify issues
- ✦ Identify opportunities for positive government changes
- ✦ Identify initiatives
- ✦ Fund initiatives
- ✦ VOTE!
- ✦ Work as a "Cyber Team" for Results

This web site is designed for you to become a voice that is heard. If we can band together and create enough noise, Washington and the States will hear us and have to take action or they will have a hard time staying in power (i.e. elected).

Social Media:

Spread the word that we need to unite by using your social media platforms. Twitter it out and let's see if we can gain just as much momentum as our government. Contribute to blogs and flood the internet with the truth. Use social media to start and continue this revolution of change for our society.

Thank you!

Thank you for reading this book. Please pass this book along to your sphere of influence. We need to get the word out that there are solutions and now is the time to act. America has been the beacon of hope for so many around the world – we cannot let our light dim or go out. May God continue to bless America.

About the Authors

John Walker is a concerned citizen. He has been in business for 22 years following a successful high school coaching and teaching career. After asking many experts and Congress people why the crisis facing America was not being solved, John spent three years investigating the roadblocks, in and outside the government, to America's recovery. These discoveries spawned common sense solutions to help America. With encouragement from his colleagues, these ideas evolved into this book. John believes that men can only apply knowledge to successful problem solving when it is accompanied by God's wisdom. His hope is that you will find wisdom as you read these pages. John has been married to Valicia for 22 years and has 2 great kids, Megan and Logan.

Kris Axhoj is also a concerned citizen. He earned an Industrial Engineering degree and spent 15 years as a systems and management consultant in corporate America. Eleven years ago Kris and his wife, Rhonda, started a construction company and have experienced the positives and negatives of operating a small business in America. Kris has studied and experimented with many types of building techniques and understands first hand the Green Movement and sustainable principles. Kris is also passionate about history and political theory. His hope is that readers will digest the information presented in this book and be motivated enough to take action resulting in a better country for our children. Kris has been married to Rhonda for 20 years and they have 3 wonderful children: Joshua, Tucker, and Jane.

Notes